SING ME TO HEAVEN

how music saved me from life's traumas

CAROLANA CALLAWAY

Sing Me to Heaven: How Music Saved Me from Life's Traumas
Copyright © 2019 by Carolana Callaway

Requests for information should be sent via e-mail to HIM Publications. Visit www.himpublications.com for contact information.

Scripture quotations are taken from the Holy Bible, New International Version®, NIV®, copyright © 1973, 1978, 1984, 2011 by Biblica, Inc.™ Used by permission of Zondervan. All rights reserved worldwide. www.zondervan.com. The "NIV" and "New International Version" are trademarks registered in the United States Patent and Trademark Office by Biblica, Inc.™

Any Internet addresses (websites, blogs, etc.) in this book are offered as a resource. They are not intended in any way to be or imply an endorsement by HIM Publications; nor does HIM Publications vouch for the content of these sites and contact numbers for the life of this book.

All rights reserved. No part of this book, including icons and images, may be reproduced in any manner without prior written permission from the copyright holder, except where noted in the text and in the case of brief quotations embodied in critical articles and reviews.

ISBN 978-1-970102-08-6 (Paperback)
ISBN 978-1-970102-09-3 (Kindle)
ISBN 978-1-970102-10-9 (ePub)

Cover and interior design: Harrington Interactive Media

Photo on dedication page from Carolana Callaway's personal collection.

Printed in the United States of America

I would like to first dedicate this book to God, my heavenly Father, because without his supernatural strength, this book would not have been possible.

And also to my earthly father, Papi (Dr. Jose Antonio La Fontaine-Thibodeaux), who taught me my first song.

Papi and Carolana

Contents

Acknowledgements 9

Foreword by Mark Cawley 11

PART I: About This Book 13

PART II: My Musical Roots 19

    1 | Lady Bass 21

    2 | Momma's Bass 27

    3 | Let the Duets Begin 31

    4 | Sing a Carol 35

PART III: Childhood Silenced 43

    5 | Snatched-Away Day 47

    6 | From Heaven to Hell 51

    7 | Swing Songs with Daddy Jesus 55

    8 | Miss Dottie 57

    9 | Learning to Hide 61

    10 | My First Guitar 65

PART IV: Life Before Multiple Sclerosis 69

    11 | Reconnection in Venezuela 71

    12 | Happiness in Venezuela 75

    13 | Homeland Lost 79

    14 | A Broken Marriage 85

    15 | Christy's Dance Home 87

    16 | Burning Feet 91

    17 | Papi Creates Survival Keys 95

    18 | The Diagnosis That Changed My Life 101

PART V: Living with Multiple Sclerosis 105

    19 | Becoming Silent and Still 109

    20 | The God of Appearing Normal 113

    21 | Just Shy of Suicide 117

    22 | My Humble Gift 121

    23 | Not to My Child! 127

    24 | The Guilt of Survival 131

    25 | Glass Houses 135

PART VI: Reconciliations 139

    26 | We'll Fly Away 141

    27 | The Gift of Dementia 147

    28 | From Fury to Forgiveness 153

    29 | A Moral Dilemma 157

30 | Missing Chromosome: An Answer 161
31 | Bethany's Legacy of Music 165

PART VII: From Survivor to Songwriter 171
32 | Songwriter's Freedom Song 175
33 | Where Do I Go From Here? 179
34 | Sing Me to Heaven 185

Timeline of Events 187
About the Author 191

Acknowledgments

I would like to thank Brian and Bethany for the times when your input and encouragement were invaluable. You lovingly held my arms up when I no longer had the strength to hold them up alone.

I would like to thank my long-time friend and writing coach Mark who always knew I could write this book—you were right!

I would like to thank Chad and Logan, because without your strength and moral support, this book may not have ever been finished and published.

Thank you Dr. Gretchen Campbell, my friend and neurologist, who has taught me the medical importance of my writing. Thank you to *all* my wonderful doctors who made sure I would still be alive today to write this book.

A very special thanks to all the empowering people who made my childhood survival possible. I'd like to thank everyone throughout my life who believed that I could survive—because I did.

Foreword

Carolana Callaway's life has been a journey—and what a journey it has been! I won't give it away because you have to experience it for yourself in these pages.

I met Carolana when I became her songwriting coach in 2015. I realized pretty quickly our sessions were about much more than words and music. She writes from a heart that's full of rich life experiences, and so much of her story has been overcoming unimaginable adversity.

After coaching her for a few years, I suggested she needed to tell her story, as a legacy piece. Like all real-life heroes, she has a quiet, inner strength that's carried her, and the stories in this book will inspire others to find their own strength for the journey. I am so happy that she's shared her story here and I'm proud to call her my friend. You need to discover these stories for yourself and trust me, you'll fall in love with this woman and come to admire her as much as I do.

—**MARK CAWLEY**, author of *Song Journey*
and hit songwriter and songwriting coach

PART I

About This Book

This book began with the notion that endorphins from my songwriting and making music would help me to heal, to always stay ahead of my Multiple Sclerosis prognosis, and to be resilient to life's difficulties. As I've written the book, though, I've realized music's effect on me is much broader than physical healing. The mental energy I spent listening to music as a child and then creating music as an adult, gave me strength to reconcile life's traumas with inner peace. No matter what I've had to go through, I've survived—even thrived—thanks to music and songwriting. Music feeds, heals, and nourishes my soul.

The stories in this book will tell my history, but my songwriting will provide an intimate glimpse into my heart and soul. My stories and songs are like conjoined twins: one cannot live without the other. They share vital creative organs that made me the person God created me to be. Both of them must be read together to know my full soul.

God-inspired songs have always carried me. They have given me the courage to survive from birth until now. They carried me through horrific childhood abuse, and even now—decades later—through the daily frustrations of an advanced terminal form of Multiple Sclerosis. The stories and songs in this book are woven together to give my heart the faith and courage to face life's sometimes-overwhelming trials. Stories, songs, and faith are the life-threads I've used to weave together my strong and courageous life tapestry. God knew where each of those threads would be in the masterfully designed fabric of my life.

For example, as a young child, I faced daily physical, emotional, and sexual abuse from my foster care parents. My bruised and broken heart would be mended by the songs I sang to myself. If there was a song I really liked, I'd make up new verses to make the song last longer. Those were my first attempts at songwriting. The time I spent as a child making up verses to calm my heart formed a foundation that now serves me well as a Nashville songwriter, and songwriting and music continue to provide me daily healing. Each time I hear God-inspired music, I feel another piece of heaven in my heart.

My stories will show the miracle of God's transformation of an abused foster child and teen mom into an international diplomat with a PhD in International Human Rights Law. While I do not think any child deserves abuse, my life is an example of how our Lord can take even abuse and use it for his purpose. My abuse taught me to care about the suffering of other victims. In the same way that songs healed my heart, I saw music heal abused hearts around the world. God's songs work musical miracles in

• About This Book •

hurting, abused hearts no matter the location or language. The Holy Bible tells us that "God so loved the world," and therefore, he loves all nations enough to send them heart-healing songs (John 3:16).

I've seen and experienced musical miracles as I've traveled throughout the world. In 2006, while on a United Nations assignment in the West African country of Ghana, my left foot became numb. In the following months, the numbness ascended up my entire left side. After months of endless misdiagnoses, a correct diagnosis was made of Marburg's Progressive Multiple Sclerosis. Marburg's MS is a cruel form of gradual disability. My life of international travel sadly ended, and with a bruised and broken heart, I sang those familiar songs from my childhood. I called them my swing songs back then, but now, instead of a swing, I rock in a chair to their heart-healing melodies. As painful as any form of MS can be, God still used my MS for his purpose. My MS became "Must Slow down" and "Must Sing." I traded my diplomatic passport for a writing notebook. I traded my airplane seat for a comfortable rocking recliner. And I traded my south Atlanta historical home for a one-room log cabin on the Tennessee River close to Nashville. My MS had become my new mantra of "Mighty Songwriter."

Writing this book is quite possibly my life's final chapter. My Marburg's MS has become advanced and very painful. My life centers around at least three major doctor's appointments a week. In the hours before dawn, I often wake up with back spasms so severe that my screams sound like they are coming from a torture chamber. These episodes occur several times a night and can last for several hours at a time. Many MS patients refer to them as MS Night Terrors. The pain provokes more physical fatigue, which then worsens the effects of MS. The only medication that can lessen them is one of the "top-shelf" narcotics such as morphine shots or surgical-level opiates. Unfortunately, those are not an option for me. My body is so exhausted that my brain doesn't send adequate nocturnal signals to my lungs. Any strong pain medication would depress those signals, and my lungs could stop working in my sleep.

The most effective medicine for my spasms is the same I used in my childhood abuse years: music! Singing in my rocking recliner or writing a song at my desk, I get the best medicine, little known by all of the great minds at Vanderbilt Medical Center. It is the healing power of a soft song. It's not the perfect voice and tune that make a song worthy of praise. It is the grateful and joyful heart that makes any noise a song worthy to praise our Lord. My daily songs of praising him allow me to peek into the endless joy of Heaven. Perhaps joy is the purpose of Heaven. You cannot have praise without joy; nor can you have joy without praise. Singing is God's way of helping Christians to practice for praising him eternally in Heaven. One thing I know for sure—Heaven is a place of endless praise and joy.

Before I make my way to Heaven, though, I needed to write this book and share my story. God has kept me on this earth much longer than my original prognosis of three to five years in 2007, and I truly believe there is a reason for that. If the stories of how I overcame struggles through the power of song can help others, my life will have had a greater purpose than I ever dreamed. It's

• About This Book •

with this intention that I leave you, Reader, with my stories and songs. I hope by the end you will feel the power of song and join in to Sing Me to Heaven!

PART II

My Musical Roots

"Sweet Little Angel Child"
By Mama Blanca Thibodeaux and Carolana Callaway
Sweet little Angel Child
You didn't know from where
You was comin'.
Oh, Sweet little Angel Child
You didn't know to who
You be belongin'.
Oh, Sweet little Angel Child
You comin' from my heart
And belongin' in my song.

My family is like an orchestra. Momma plays the bass, Papi plays the piano and fiddle, Mama Blanca sings in her deep alto tenor voice, Aunt Tibby sings the high notes, and I fill in with a guitar, the mandolin, the lyrics, and my own soulful voice adding to the chorus. We are a symphony, a harmony, a choir of genetics and history that bonds us together through music. We sing gospel on Sunday morning, we groove to R&B on Saturday night, and we dance and holler together to Cajun zydeco any day of the week.

Though many of the orchestra members have passed on, the orchestra is still alive in my musical DNA.

My parents are examples of our family's connection to music, which goes beyond mere talent or skill. Their connection to music is part of the family's very existence. For example, Momma played bass and was the lead singer of her own R&B band in New Orleans in the late 50s. Papi was working at the Alabama Trade Center in Mobile as a Venezuelan Consulate at the time but was passionately looking to play the fiddle in a band. He would get home each day, jump out of his three-piece suit and into jeans and boots, and head down to The Big Easy to try and pick up a gig. One day he fiddled his way into Momma's band, and from there my history began.

Though I don't know much about my parents' family histories, the stories that follow have been passed down to me by word of mouth and through journals. Of all the examples throughout my family's history of our ability to survive hardship through the music that lives within our souls, the story of Lady Bass is where the Survival Power of Music is most evident.

1

Lady Bass

The story of "Lady Bass" shows how full my family history is with the life-giving power of music. This story came to me from my distant cousin Pierre on my Papi's side of the family, la Fontaines. Pierre found it in one of my mother's journals kept by my father's sister, Aunt Tibby. She was a prolific record keeper and kept everything about our family history. When I reconnected with her as an adult, she still had all my baby pictures and baby albums, and even invitations to Momma's baby shower for me. The only reason I can think of for Papi's sister having my mother's journals is that Momma must have kept them at Papi's house when she was traveling the circuit to New Orleans in the R&B and bluegrass music scene. Momma probably left her journals with Papi and Aunt Tibby because she knew her ex-husband would destroy anything involving music that she brought to his house. When Momma went back to her ex-husband, Aunt Tibby kept her journals. Among my mother's things that Aunt Tibby had kept, Pierre found a group of journals written by my maternal great-grandfather, Jean Louis la Fontaine (the family called him "Lilo").

Jean Louis was a relatively well-known cellist and bass fiddler troubadour in France during World War I. One night, there was a bombing of a Belgium theater during a concert. Jean Louis was at the theater with his bass fiddle. The bomb landed in the middle of the performance hall, killing many of the attendees instantly, and the orchestra's striking Rococo Victorian Concert Grand piano was crushed under the debris. In his journal, my great-grandfather described how the marble of the walls became pebbles and the velvet curtains were torn asunder. He wrote, with the pen of a poet, that he wondered if that was what the veil looked like when it was ripped in two after the death of Christ.

His friend Claude played in the symphony for that particular concert. He was a coffin maker by trade. He had made a box for my great-grandfather's bow—I still have it, and it looks like a little coffin. It's lined with wallpaper and the wood has a dark stain.

The chaos that ensued after the bombing engulfed the theater. Those who were not killed or crushed by the rubble hunkered down, nursed their injuries, and waited out the city-wide bombing. They had to stay silent or the enemy troops shouting in the streets might have searched what remained of the theater and killed the survivors. So they were trapped and forced to live in the theater's rubble for weeks while the city around them burned. They ate what supplies the theater had, but they basically starved while waiting for weeks of fighting to pass.

Due to divine providence, Claude and my great-grandfather and his bass survived the bombing and found each other. There was some damage to the bass, but nothing like what happened to the baby grand piano. Claude and Jean Louis decided to make a coffin case for the bass out of the piano's remains. Jean Louis was planning to leave for America, but Claude was injured and too weak to travel. He told my great-grandfather, "Let me send myself with you by making this case for your Lady Bass."

Claude used hinging and wood from the destroyed piano to make the case, and they used shards and chunks of marble for tools. To keep silent and hidden, they would set the tools, nails, and materials on the ground so that when the fighting grew loud nearby, they could time their hammering with the rhythm of the machine guns outside. Everything was laid out and ready for them to work undetected.

As they worked and their cabin fever grew, they would talk about the bass. They said things like, "She is a lovely lady. What a lovely waist on such a lovely lady. Every lovely lady deserves to attend a gala in the United States of America." They cut a belt from the curtain trimmings and wrapped the Lady in the remaining curtains as padding, commenting that the Lady Bass was now dressed for her gala. In his life, my great-grandfather attracted many women, but they always fell away when they realized he only had one lady in his life: Lady Bass.

Jean Louis was particularly heartbroken that the dust and debris from the explosion were lodged in the cracks and crevices of the bass. He took the strings from the piano that corresponded to the bass and he cleaned them for days using pieces of velvet cloth from the curtains.

He joked in his journal entry, "And now, for the first time, we may be able to play a piano and a bass fiddle ensemble with just one instrument."

When it was finally safe to leave, my great-grandfather gathered some food in a bundle and went to the dock with Lady Bass to travel to America, but the captain told him he could not bring the large case on board. He may have been scared that there was an actual coffin with a body inside, or he may have just been spooked by it. Either way, he wasn't letting it on his ship.

My great-grandfather was stubborn, though. The captain finally relented and said, "Look, the only way you can take that box on my ship is if you stay with it in the cargo hold. You must leave everything else because you will not be a passenger. You have to sleep with the box and stay with it for the whole trip."

This was not a modern-day cruise ship. You had to bring your own food for the two-month journey—people would starve if they didn't bring enough food. Louis had to make a decision between his meager rations of food and Lady Bass. He threw down his bundle and waltzed onto the ship with the bass.

He spent the trip in sometimes blinding darkness surrounded by rats. (It's a wonder he didn't get the plague). The cargo hold was pitch black except for the slight light coming through the deck grate from the sky far above him.

After some time, he decided to take Lady Bass out of her case and play her at night. As my great-grandfather wrote in his journal, Lady Bass cast her spell on the travelers of the ship. He wrote,

"Out of nowhere, food fell from heaven. I never went a day without a nibble." Whenever he played, people began dropping morsels of food down to him. Sometimes even a portion of wine would be lowered by rope. Nobody had very much food. Everyone was starving, but they shared enough that he survived.

"All of a sudden, my music had a whole new purpose," he wrote. "Before then, music helped my soul survive because it was who I was. But now, I had to literally play for my supper." He talked about the few times he fell ill with what he called "boat illness" and wasn't able to play. On those days, he wouldn't have food. But once he began playing again, a morsel would be sent down once more.

Had he not played, I would not be here. Because of music, he was literally able to stay alive. That is the survival power of music.

When he realized they were approaching land, he attempted to comb his hair with his bow. Since he was considered cargo, he was one of the last things to leave the ship. Before he left the galley, he made sure Lady Bass looked her very best for her welcoming gala. She was almost a real person to him by that point. He had to look presentable, too—he was French, after all. He was very weak by then, and when he went to tighten his belt he was shocked to find the belt could circle him twice. Rather than pleated, his pants were gathered. He had probably been living off a biscuit or a chunk of cheese a day.

Jean Louis opened the bass's coffin-like case on the deck and stood Lady Bass up proudly against the rail of the ship. He said to her, "Lady Bass, may I present Lady Liberty. May you always be the best of friends."

Several times Pierre and I have wept while reading the poetic writings of our great-grandfather.

Aunt Tibby left so many documents, and left them in disarray, so we are still trying to sort through them to find out what happened next. The next information I know for sure is that my mother carried around Lady Bass as a child, and it's that bass that jump-started her career.

Momma's Bass

My momma got her start with Lady Bass at the young age of fourteen. This was a time when girls married and had children young, so she was already engaged to a man named Charles Foster, who disapproved of her playing. Not only did Charles refuse to see her play but also when he let her play at all, he would make her walk alone at night down Finley Avenue, one of the most dangerous streets in town, to go perform. This was also before base cases had wheels and straps. Petite but strong-willed, Momma had to carry Lady Bass all the way to the music hall, strapping the bass onto her back with men's belts and carrying it like a turtle shell. This didn't bother her, though—she was going to play music.

She went to the same hall day after day to try to play with the band there, but the leader kept telling her, "You're a little lady, and ladies don't play in bands." He let her sing every now and then but never let her in as a regular.

She showed up to rehearsal one day, and they weren't playing. When she asked why, she was told that one of the members, Carl, had dropped dead from a massive heart attack. She asked, "Will the band play?" They were unsure.

She asked if she could play, and the leader said to her, "Little lady, the only way I'll let you in the band is if you can go up there and play Carl's bass."

This small girl put her hands on her hips and said, "I'll have you know I've been playing one bigger than that since I was four and could stand on a stool to play it."

The band members laughed and the leader said, "Well, get her a stool."

My mother stood up on that stool and played that bass. They let her join the band.

One of her old band members told me much later, "We always knew when Ginny Lee was coming down the street because we could hear her clod-hoppers." They called them this because the soles of her shoes were always coming loose from the top of her shoe, and they would clank as she walked.

My mother had four children with Charles before she separated from him and before she gave birth to me. Charles was abusive and controlling, and he did everything he could to prevent her from playing her music. But my mother was used to abuse—she had been abused by her stepfather as a child, too.

When my mother finally gathered all of her courage and left Charles, she began the process of filing for a divorce and went to live with her youngest sister and brother-in-law in Slidell, Louisiana.

She travelled the circuit between New Orleans, Biloxi, and Mobile under the name Ginny Lee. Sometimes they might play all three towns in one day. Even after a full day of performing, they had to break down their sound equipment and lock away their instruments. But Momma was popular in New Orleans and often got to stay there for several nights in a row. During one of her New Orleans layovers, she met my father who played the fiddle. They ended up getting together, and she became pregnant with me. When I was born, my mother's grandmother, whom I called "Mama Blanca," moved in to help take care of me. The first few years of my life living with Momma, Papi, and Mama Blanca were the happiest of my childhood.

3

Let the Duets Begin

Music surrounded me from my earliest childhood memories in Ocean Springs, Mississippi. My heart was formed and filled with music that gives my life an enduring rhythm—even when the world around me is off beat.

My musical roots with Papi go back to before I could sit up on my own. It's said that he would hold me sitting next to him on the couch. He'd sing to me, and I would try to sing with him with my baby mimicking sounds until my head would fall over hard asleep. He would laugh so hard he'd either wake me or almost drop me.

My first fiddle was a 1/64 Papi gave me not long after I started to walk. A 1/64 is the smallest fiddle made, about the size of an adult hand. Standing in front of the giant dressing room mirror with Papi standing behind me, I tried so hard to hold my fiddle just like he did his.

He would joyfully yell, "Let the duets begin!"

My tiny hands would work vigorously to squeak out a tune, my bow popping me in the face. The loud squeaking made us both laugh. There was no harmony, but it was music because the sounds gave us joy. It was no masterpiece, but it was a laughter-piece, which in many ways is just as good.

During these early years my great-grandmother, Mama Blanca, would daily hum me to sleep at nap time with the first songs I remember. She sang sweet and slow to the rhythm of her rocking chair as it cracked back and forth on the antique wooden floor. When I pressed my ear against her chest, I could hear that her voice came from a deeper place—it came from her heart. The songs were old black spirituals that she sang in her native Creole French. Her deep, longing voice echoed the sufferings of her West African ancestors. Her thick Creole accent added sparkle to the tapestry of her low contralto voice.

The stained glass trim above my bedroom windows let sunlight create dancing rainbows on my wall. Those rainbows seemed to come alive only when Mama Blanca sang. When she sang to me, she lifted me to the clouds, and my little room became a piece of heaven. As she rocked me, I breathed in the sunny fragrance of Ariel detergent from the snow-white curtain dancing in the breeze.

Just outside the windows came song-like chants from the open market vendors. Above the voices, I could hear Mama Blanca's husband, nicknamed "Happy Jack," calling from his corner Haitian market. Long before I could read, I knew his store by the sound of his happy chanting charming potential customers. Even when he talked, his words streamed out in a type of soft harmony tone. And when he walked, it was with the movement of a soft-shoe dancer. When we brought home Ariel detergent, it was like we brought a little bag of Happy Jack home with us. And when Mama Blanca wore the scent of Ariel, it seemed as if I could touch the sunshine. I didn't simply hear music all around me—I could smell it with every breath I took, and it became part of my soul.

My nap time began with the music of Mama Blanca's singing, but I always awoke to the sound of Papi's piano. He would come home for his lunch break and sit down at his piano in the parlor to fill the house with his playing. Our house in Ocean Springs had a courtyard atrium in the center of the bottom floor, and all the upstairs bedrooms surrounded it. Music from anywhere in the house would float into the atrium and up to all the bedrooms.

Sometimes I would rush down the stairs to the parlor and Papi would pick me up to stand on the bench so I could reach the keys. Laying my hands on his hands, he guided my fingers up and down the keyboard. Afterwards we would clap together, enjoying being both the players and the audience. The way Papi played felt like a language between us.

My entire family was musical, but it was Papi who taught me the power of music. His love and devotion, so much of the time expressed in song and music, taught me how to get through a difficult childhood after I was taken away from him and put with a foster family. The core values of a loving family were intimately entwined with my soul's need to hold onto music.

I still have his 125-year-old piano, and you can see on the ivory of the keys little chips from where I literally cut my teeth gnawing on the piano as Papi played, tasting the music. Even now, I can replay Mama Blanca's voice on the haunting black keys of Papi's piano in the key of A minor and be brought back to this heavenly time of my childhood. Anytime my heart takes my mind back to them, I realize that even though Mama Blanca and Papi are no longer with me, they can still Sing Me to Heaven.

4

Sing a Carol

My Papi only shared with me one story of his time in the horrific concentration camp Auschwitz I. Out of that "death camp" came a miraculous birth, which is connected, across the decades, to my own name.

In late 1943, the German Nazi SS marched into Northern Italy in search of Jews and Jewish sympathizers. One of their first stops was in my father's hometown of Tivoli. At thirteen, my Papi, his twin brother Jose Francisco ("Cisco"), and his mother Maria Elizabet Saraiva-Tivoli ("Lita") became actively involved in an underground movement to help Jewish children. They were part of a system of smuggling children from Germany through Italy to escape to the South American country of Venezuela. Once the children arrived, they were officially adopted into awaiting Venezuelan families.

Being of Jewish descent themselves, my family was caught by the Nazis and sent to concentration camps. Papi and his brother were sent to Auschwitz because they were twins and a Nazi researcher named Mengele was calling for twins for his experiments.

Decades later, my Papi and his mother, Lita, carried a constant reminder of their time in the camps. Their prisoner ID numbers were tattooed on their forearms. I'm not sure when or how the SS captured them, nor did they ever speak of the release from Auschwitz, but both Papi and his mother made attempts to hide their shameful tattoos by wearing long sleeves even on the hottest of summer days. Occasionally, one of their tattoos would accidentally be exposed, and an ice-cold stillness would come over both of their faces. They had an emotionally vacant stare that told me they shared memories so horrific that no words exist to describe the nightmares. Their stares would press onto the room a momentary but heavy silence that seemed like it lasted a lifetime. That's the kind of sentiment they carried with them about their time in concentration camps. That's why I was surprised at what happened just before Papi's death, on Christmas of 1992.

My Papi had finally found the courage to tell me just one Holocaust story. It was the story of how my name was connected to his time in Auschwitz. Reliving painful memories, he began:

> *Most Italians were kept in concentration camps inside Italy, but once it was discovered that Cisco and I were twins, we were snatched up and shipped off to a barracks—Auschwitz's Block 10. Prisoners in Block 10 were medical guinea pigs. Because we were darker than the northern Europeans, we were labeled Gypsies. We felt so degraded by that label. Cisco and I had once been heirs of a very proud, powerful Italian family. But now, we did well to have more than a pajama top to wear. We were*

forced to sleep six to a bunk-shelf. The barracks and bed-shelves were made from rustic wood, the same type of wood used to make animal stables. I felt like an animal—really more like a creature. I lived off a daily bowl of watered-down turnip soup. My family's sheep had more daily food than I was given.

Cisco and I struggled to learn the languages spoken inside the barracks, but most nights were spent in silence out of respect for the medically mangled. I want to believe that Cisco died in Auschwitz from a complication of his Lupus that he had suffered with since birth. But like Cisco, many were taken and never returned to the barracks.

Block 10 sat next to the "medical care" building. Screaming became our daily serenade. At daybreak we were paraded outside for roll call, and I could hear the crunch of footsteps on the frozen ground in front of that building. When the footsteps had an uneven rhythm, I knew it was a pregnant lady being taken inside for another madman's medical experiment. The pregnant women were taken inside at daybreak, but during nighttime roll call they never came back out. At night, there was only the stench of death, coming from a rusty oil-barrel where unborn babies had been tossed out like common trash. I tried to focus on the stars and ignore the smell of the little lives lost to that rusty barrel.

Being a Catholic, I cried and prayed nightly for the salvation of the souls of those mothers and their tossed-away children. I always prayed that by some miracle one of the babies might live.

More death seemed to be the only answer to my prayers.

The winter got colder, and the air was filled with Christmas carols from the SS officers' parties. The first Christmas was filled with hope by the miraculous birth of the Baby Jesus, but this Christmas was filled with death—even before birth. Each night, I prayed longer and harder to the Blessed Mother for another Christmas miracle: Please just let one of those tossed-away babies live!

With the SS soldiers drunk from too much Christmas partying, we prisoners had more liberties at night. One night, I slipped out to see the Christmas stars and tried to forget the constant horrors. Halfway between the barracks and the medical building, I thought I heard a baby's muffled cry. It was so weak that I couldn't be sure if it was indeed a baby or some trapped animal. Careful to follow in the packed snow of other's footprints, I sneaked to the backdoor of the medical barracks. To my surprise, inside that rusty barrel was a baby girl barely crying. Christmas of 1944 had come for me—I had my miracle! I frantically dug her out of the barrel and ran with her to my barracks. I stood just inside the doorway and took her from under my filthy shirt. The entire barracks froze in silence. From far in the distance, we heard church chimes playing "Silent Night." An older prisoner took off his pajama pants so we could wrap the baby. Another boy began to put drops of turnip soup in her mouth. Hope and joy filled our barracks! A little child had been born in this place of death!

Each of us sang "Silent Night" in our own language as the distant Christmas chimes played. Finally, we could all understand one language—a helpless baby's cry. Love for that baby was the language we all grew to understand. She brought us together in a common cause for hope. Her cries became our personal Christmas carol, so she was named Carol.

Our daily goal was to keep Carol alive. We would take turns drinking our own urine to make us vomit. If we were vomiting, it was assumed that we had cholera, and none of the guards wanted us near them. Vomiting meant you could stay inside and take care of little Carol.

As winter went on, the church chimes stopped, and the crunch of icy snow grew louder. Some prisoners were losing fingers and toes from frostbite as winter grew colder. But somehow little Christmas Carol was surviving. She was a miracle!

One day, I was very sick and didn't need to drink urine to vomit. I had vomited all night and by daybreak was barely alive. I cuddled Carol close to me and admired her big green eyes. Behind her eyes, I could always see hope. I was so faint that I fell asleep watching her.

The burning slap of an SS guard awoke me. Carol had been crying! I had failed to keep her quiet! The dreadful SS guards had discovered her. One of them snatched Carol from my arms and slammed her against the wall to her death. Her lifeless body was hurled into the toss-away barrel. I hugged the little wet spot she had made on my shirt. I wept as I promised her that somehow, someday, I would avenge her death.

I carried that guilt until the day you were born, Carolana. I watched your premature body barely holding onto life. You were so sick with tubes running all over your body. Your frightened mother had left you all alone just like little Christmas Carol. Your chances for survival were very low, but through all the tubes I saw your eyes. So big! So bright! So hopeful! I knew you were my chance to avenge Christmas Carol's death. You weren't a Christmas baby, but you were my own personal miracle.

That night I walked out and saw the stars in the sky. They were the same stars that shined the night I discovered Christmas Carol. Later that night, the nurses allowed me to hold you. You were in so much pain from all the tubes and needles. As I held you, I sang the one song I knew you needed, "Silent Night," and you quietly fell asleep. I said to you, "Sleep in heavenly peace—my little Carolana—my heart's little song."

Hearing this story, I realized it was no accident that my name stemmed from a song, a carol. Carols helped my Papi survive the Holocaust, and he named me Carolana to pass that power on to me. Before I was even born, I was destined to survive all my hardships through the power of music.

PART III

Childhood Silenced

"Daddy Jesus"
By Carolana Callaway
Daddy Jesus, won't you please,
Lay my head down on your knees.
You care every time I cry,
Rock me to our lullaby.
Daddy Jesus, through my tears,
Whisper our song into my ear.
And every time I hear our song,
Your words help me be real strong.

One day I was happily playing with my biological family, but by dark, I was going to bed with my foster family. My world seemed to end in less than twenty-four hours. Before getting into my experience, I must note that many of the names from my childhood have been changed. My foster family will be referred to as the Fosters instead of their real family name, and everyone within that family will have a fictitious name. I do this because this book is not about indicting my abusers, it's about the story of surviving thanks to the power of music. The effects of abuse last a lifetime, but I hope in describing my experience I am aiding in the breaking of the cycle.

While I have vivid memories of being in foster care, a lot of information I now have about my transition to foster care was given to me decades after the fact in small bits from members of my family and community. I know now that my mother's husband Charles set up the demise of our family. Charles couldn't stand how my mother had left him and had me, a child out of wedlock. Charles was set on breaking Momma, and he took her to court for custody rights of her children.

Charles used two things against Momma in court: She had a couple of her black relatives in her band, and she had lost two previous children to sickness. Given the culture of discrimination against black people, Momma didn't look like a fit mother on paper to the southern judge.

When Papi found out I'd been taken to Juvenile Hall to await foster-care placement, he showed up at court disheveled and irate, demanding my release. Being a foreigner, he had no rights. Policemen took him out of the court by the arms, and I didn't see him again until I was grown. He was told by Charles and his family that if he reached out to me, they would take out a restraining order against him or have him put in jail. He worried for my safety, so he kept his distance.

After the custody hearing, my father tried to commit suicide three times in a weekend because he'd lost the love of his life and his only child. He had a big scar on his head from when he had crushed a sherry glass against a fireplace and sliced his face.

He never remarried and never had any other children as far as I know. He suffered in his loss of Momma and me. He had even offered to adopt all my mother's children and take us all to Venezuela so he wouldn't lose me. But as often happens in abusive relationships, even though my mother considered this, she was addicted to her abuser. Once her music, her children, and my dad were taken away, she had no strength left. She was lost.

When I was an adult, Papi told me that it seemed like the better he was to my mother, the more she feared him. The more her fans cheered her, the more frightened she became. Her life of abuse distorted her understanding of love and of her music. Music and love were entwined with abuse. I, too, struggled with this distorted thinking due to my own experience with abuse after being torn from my family and put into an abusive situation.

5

Snatched-Away Day

Excessive performing, songwriting, and having seven babies in as many years pushed Momma to drug addiction. The more life demanded of her, the more drugs she needed just to keep going each day. As her career spiraled upward, her addiction spiraled her life downward. As her world crumbled, though, she managed to keep my small world perfect.

I remember being wrapped up in her arms in a fluffy towel when I was about four, swaddled like Baby Jesus. I would be wet and cold, and my skin would be pruned and shriveled from a bath time gone too long, but the sound of my mother's voice would fill me with warm love. She could wipe away the cold with a song. As she swirled me down the hallway to our bedroom, she would say, "Let's go play puff-puff."

Bouncing onto the bed, squealing with delight, I would ready myself for "puffing." Momma had a favorite purple powder puff from the dime store she'd use to powder me from head to toe with lilac-fragrant talc powder. We sang the Hokey Pokey together, and changed the words to: "Puff your right toe now ... puff your left hand now … puff under-neck now … and shake it all about." My whole body would be as white as baking flour. I giggled and coughed—I loved it. I was playing with Momma!

We would both slip into our sleeping slips, the powder ensuring we'd wake up with no chafing. I loved to jump under the covers to warm a place in the cold sheets for Momma. I twisted the covers around me like a little Eskimo baby with just my eyes peeking out. I watched my mom brush her long, dark, curly hair. She looked like a princess to me. Peace filled our little kingdom.

Suddenly, our peaceful world was shattered. The sirens, bright lights, and banging at our front door filled me with terror. A loud voice shouted, "Virginia Foster, we know you are in there! We've come to take the little girl! Bring her out now!" Momma's face froze with fear. Her eyes glazed over in shock. She grabbed her red-checkered waist-dress and fumbled to dress herself. Shouts and kicks at the door seemed deafening in my tiny ears. I began to scream, but Momma grabbed me up and said, "Hold on to me tight! Not a hug, child—but choke me around the neck with your little arms." She began sobbing as she whispered, "If we hold each other tight enough, no one can ever separate us!"

The police had loosened the front door hinges with their pounding. When Momma opened the front door, the rusty, warped screened door fell to the porch floor with a bang. One of the policemen read words from a blue sheet of paper. I didn't understand them, but worst of all, Momma didn't either. She stood there in a daze, clutching me tightly.

A strange lady dressed in a pillbox hat with a matching suit reached out to take me from Momma, but Momma turned me away from her. She squeezed me so tight I could feel her tears fall on my cheeks and then onto my lips. I could taste the salt in her tears. She pressed me into her chest so that I could barely breathe, but I felt comforted by the smell of her lilac powder. I wanted so desperately to run back inside and continue our game of "puff-puff."

Momma began to rock me back and forth. She muttered the words of my favorite lullaby she had written and sung to me hundreds of times before.

> **"Mommy's Lullaby"**
> *By My Mommy and Me*
> I loved you then
> I love you now
> I'll love you
> When life pulls us apart.
> Each night I'll come
> In your dreams
> I'll come and sing
> To heal our broken hearts.

Even though Momma had written our song and I had heard it so many times before, I barely recognized it. Fear had shocked her voice. I'd never seen her so afraid. I'd never heard her scream so loud. If someone as great as Momma was afraid, then I must really be doomed.

The strange pillbox hat lady yelled at Momma, "You must give us the child! She is not safe with you!" Their shouts of other long words I didn't understand came at my ears like the chilling noises of a horror house. A policeman reached forward and snatched me away from Momma's arms. He dragged me down the steps and whirled me into the backseat of a giant, red car with lights flashing on top.

I sat in that strange, giant car alone. I cried until my cheeks burned and my lips bled from nervous biting. The seats were covered in a raised bubble design and made raw spots on the back of my legs. I wanted my favorite yellow "Sweet N' Sassy" swirly dress on. I wanted my lacy white socks and my black Mary-Jane shoes for my freezing feet. In all the snatching me around, no one had noticed my blanket had been dropped and left behind. Instead, I only had on a thin white slip that was soaked from Momma's tears. I felt wet and cold—right down to my heart. This thin slip was all I had to face a horrific world on my own. The last I saw of Momma as we drove away was her standing alone on the porch in her own crumpled slip, weeping and rocking and singing to herself.

6

From Heaven to Hell

Shocked with fear a five-year-old shouldn't have to feel, I didn't speak to anyone for the entire time I was at Shelby County Juvenile Hall after I was taken from Momma. My only world consisted of a long, dark, haunted room called a dormitory. My tiny bed seemed dwarfed compared to the dozen other cots on which the preteens and teenagers slept. I slept and played in the same dirty, smelly dress I'd been given to wear over my slip.

Every night, one of the big boys came to tuck me in. Only, they always wanted to play with my body. The big girls would watch and giggle. I always felt so filthy and sticky after they "played" with me. During the day, I crept to a corner and tried not to be seen. If I didn't talk, then maybe they wouldn't notice me. Eventually, I pushed my bed into that same corner where my only friend became a tiny window. It gave my mind a safe place to go and escape from the hell in which I was living. I lived in silence without singing, without music, without love.

Meal time came, and an oily-haired "playmate" teenage boy brought me a red booster seat with an elephant painted on the back. The red booster seat lifted me to be tall at the table. Now I was giant, red, and again had bubbled imprints on my legs. Each mealtime, that red booster seat triggered a silent memory—and my heart was afraid. Each day, my heart felt like it was being snatched away from Momma's arms over and over again. I realized this must be what fear really feels like!

Little did I know when I was picked up by my new foster family that the fear had only just begun.

When I was placed in the care of my step-father's extended family, I was told to call my foster parents "Mom" and "Dad." I did as I was told, but they were no parents to me. As an adult, I chose to stop calling Annie "Mom" and begin calling her "Maude," a handle of authority that doesn't mean I respect you or like you but I acknowledge your authority as a senior.

From day one, I was abused by both Maude Annie and her husband physically, sexually, emotionally, and mentally. Their abuse broke me down little by little over time. I remember specifically one morning when I was dressing for school and Maude Annie came into my room and began to tear at my clothes and grab at my skin. I struggled against her and fumbled out of my room and into the living room. Maude Annie had pulled my dress almost off of me and I was exposed to my foster father, who was sitting in a chair with a paper and staring at me. This moment encompassed every kind of abuse, and it left me feeling stripped to the bone.

Even Christmas didn't feel sacred or safe while I was with my foster parents. If anything, it felt worse because they (the extended family) would gather in their enormous, rambling house. The partying would lead to silent, secret acts. Since I was my mother's illegitimate child, I was fair game. There was no one to fight for me or care enough to stop things from going too far. No one was going to protect me, so I would just have to do my best to avoid the worst of them. Christmas should have been a time for happiness and celebrating Jesus' birth, but instead it was a hell full of fear and hiding.

My foster parents sent my heart the message that I was nobody's child and that nobody wanted me. Like an indentured servant, I had no personhood. I was told I was the product of my mother's prostitution. I was told no one knew who my father really was and that my mother wouldn't have known who he was either. When I talked back, I felt afraid of the consequences.

I was drawn to the piano my foster family owned because it reminded me of my Papi. I longed to hear piano music, to relive my Papi's music. I must have believed that the piano music would guide me back to the feelings of love I had once known and that if I forgot the music, I might forget Papi.

I crept to the piano whenever I thought I was alone. I had to be careful because if someone heard me playing, my fingers would be held on the keys while the lid was slammed shut on my knuckles. My hands are deformed now from being broken in that lid. Not only did they crush my fingers over and over again, they also crushed my dreams. I was punished for happiness—anything that brought me joy was turned against me. When the abuse became so hard and I felt so much pain in my heart that it was too much, I switched to the survival mode that made thinking about being loved too frivolous to indulge my time. I had to exist without feeling. If I avoided music, I could avoid the pain of losing love.

School was no better. Since I didn't speak English well, I was considered a slow learner and thought to have a speech problem (regardless of the fact that I already spoke three other languages and could read at the age of four). Because I was not like everyone else, people seemed to believe that I had some strange, incurable disease. I spent my early years behind a screen away from the other children in the classroom. It wasn't until another foreign student joined the class that I felt less isolated.

My foster parents made me feel intimidated and afraid. They taught my soul how to be sad time and time again. Because of them I couldn't play music, I couldn't dance, I couldn't walk correctly, and I couldn't feel loved.

When I became an adult, my Aunt Tibby related my experience to my Papi's experience at Auschwitz: "Being in a concentration camp was like losing your soul. The whole idea of abuse is to take away the person's identity so they can be controlled. Did your foster family really do anything so different to you?"

7

Swing Songs with Daddy Jesus

For reasons I still don't understand, in spite of my foster parents' cruelty toward me, they did take me to church. Whatever their social motivations were for being there, I was there, and I learned to sing about Jesus. The more I sang about this Jesus who loved me, the more I grew to love him back. Learning to love him gave me faith in his power to perform miracles for me!

After each daily beating, my foster mother would collapse into a drunken slumber. Then I would escape to an old, rusty swing set to meet Jesus and sing to myself. I had learned to love two things: my swing and my Jesus. I would often sing to myself in French, and if Maude Annie heard me, she would beat me in the mouth for it. Still to this day I have a chipped tooth from one of those beatings. My jaw would be sore and my lips would bleed, and I wouldn't even understand why certain songs made her so angry. She would scream at me, "Stop talking like a baby! None of that baby language!" Little did she know it was French and not nonsense. I didn't even know the song was French, though. I just knew the song.

Going to meet Jesus, I should have been freshly bathed and dressed in my Sunday's best, smelling like sweet talcum powder with a Holy Bible clutched in my hands. Instead, I wore the same dirty dress that I had slept in for several nights in a row, my hair was ratty, I was bruised, often bleeding, and tears made trails through the dirt caked on my face. The only book I took with me was the hymnal engraved on my heart.

Somehow I just knew that Jesus would accept me for however I looked, and he would be whatever I needed him to be for me each day. Some days I would feel so lonely for my real Daddy. That's when Jesus became like a father figure to me. I called him Daddy Jesus. I didn't realize he was God's Son; all I knew about Jesus was that he was a kind man. That's all I needed to know to call him Daddy Jesus. Some days I would be so weak and crushed that I felt Jesus settle my head on his knees to soothe my heart. Often, I didn't feel anyone was left in my world to love me, but then Jesus would cause my heart to murmur the song "Jesus Loves Me." "Jesus loves me, this I know ... Little ones to him belong; they are weak but he is strong."

Never underestimate how a young child learns faith. My swing songs caused my faith to grow. All my suffering as a severely abused child made Daddy Jesus so much more real to me. My faith is not based in any religious education I received, but rather in the intimate feeling that my heart could touch Jesus and that he was there for me when it seemed like I had almost no one else to lean on.

8

Miss Dottie

In the midst of all the pain I experienced from my foster family's abuse, there was one saint who changed my life and brought me back to music: Miss Dottie.

Miss Dottie and her family were heavily involved in the church we attended. She was the leader of a children's group called The Girl's Auxiliary (GA). The GA's gave young girls the opportunity to study about foreign missions at a local Baptist church. The theme song of GA was "We've a Story to Tell the Nations" because of its focus on world topics and other nations. It was comforting to me, I think, because as a baby there were always people from other cultures and different countries coming through our house. Inadvertently, I think I associated Miss Dottie with that atmosphere of compassion and acceptance because she reminded me that there was a world outside of the Foster prison.

Miss Dottie was the first and only person I ever saw who stood up to Maude Annie. There wasn't a bullying bone in Miss Dottie's frail body, but her golden heart made her strong. I had just gotten a horrible beating from my Maude Annie and was sent outside to play. The blood ran down my legs, creating a paste with the dirt in my shoes. Pieces of rock and sticks were stuck to my legs, and the bruises were already turning purple. I had stubbed one of my toes hard on a tree root trying to dodge her blows in a "survival dance" away from her.

Miss Dottie was walking by our house and saw me in the yard. She stopped and asked me, "Aren't you going to GA today?"

"I don't think so. Mom's not feeling well."

Annie would always feign a headache after beating me. I did want to go to GA, though, because I loved the songs. I could learn the songs, and no one could take them from me. It was something I could own and it was something over which I had control. Singing with GA gave my heart hope, something I rarely felt anywhere else at this point in my life.

"Here, honey, take my hand. Maybe you and I can make Mrs. Foster feel better." She walked beside me as I struggled slowly up the 12 steps to the house.

Once inside in the dining room, she said to Annie, "Carolana really wants to go to GA; she loves to sing the songs." Miss Dottie took my hand and led me back to the kitchen while saying I was in no shape to go outside. Looking back as an adult, I think she was implying she could report Annie's abuse. Of course, back then nobody would listen to a report like that. Not even the police would step in and meddle. People didn't meddle in family business.

Maude Annie said she wasn't feeling well, but Miss Dottie replied, "Well, we need Carolana's voice today in GA." She had gotten a basin and filled it with warm water and soap, and had sat me back down at the dining room table. She took off my sandals and put my legs in the basin and washed my feet and legs with a washcloth. It was the sweetest, warmest water I'd ever felt in my life.

As she washed me, she said, "Mrs. Foster, I know it's summer time, but this child is going to need some knee socks. Go get me some knee socks, and a clean dress while you're at it."

I watched in shock as Maude Annie walked upstairs and, after a minute, brought down the clothing. I had never seen Annie follow someone else's orders before. Miss Dottie hadn't even raised her voice! She just used a firm voice and gave directions, and Annie followed them. Miss Dottie was intent on taking me to church and she made it happen.

Miss Dottie wrapped the toe I'd busted on a tree root and pulled the tall knee socks over my cuts and bruises. When she put my sandals over my socked feet, I thought it was funny-looking, until I noticed my toe beginning to bleed through. Miss Dottie changed out my shoes for some sneakers and then pulled off my dirty dress and put on my pink and white striped dress, my favorite.

Finally I was ready, and we went to GA together. This day changed my life because for the first time since I'd been taken from my father, someone showed that they cared about me and loved me.

I truly believe Miss Dottie's care inspired me to go into missionary work later. Still to this day, when I think of Christian love, I always think of Miss Dottie washing my bloody legs and feet and taking me to church when she could have easily looked the other way just like everyone else. Instead, she went out of her way to be the first person to really show my heart how to sing again. I learned how to sing and how to keep in my heart the songs I learned, which ended up serving me well in life, even in situations where I had to learn how to hide.

9

Learning to Hide

My passion for human rights began near our family's summer home in Selma, Alabama, in the summer of 1965, when the Freedom March turned into Bloody Friday. I didn't know what was happening when we pulled into town. We usually stopped at the Winn-Dixie across the street from the Hill's grocer. This time, though, Hill's had a deal for a dozen cans of Chek Cola for a dollar, and Winn-Dixie sold ten for a dollar, so we went over to Hill's. I had a little doll with me, Betsy Wetsy, wrapped in a washcloth blanket tied up with a ribbon.

When we came out of Hill's, I heard singing mixed with screaming. Just a block or so away, men and women were marching for their rights and singing, "We shall overcome!" Police turned fire hoses on them until the protesters' skin was nearly ripped away, and then they let loose the German shepherds on them. As I listened and tried to understand what was happening, a Nana and little girl rushed across the street toward me and away from police officers, and the Nana fell. The Nana reminded me of my Mama Blanca and fear tore at my heart. The little girl screamed as a policeman picked her up by her hair. She screamed that she didn't want her ribbons messed up as they had been a present from her momma. When she was thrown down, her ribbons taken from her out of spite, I went to her and gave Betsy's washcloth to the Nana to wipe the girl's face. I handed the little girl the ribbon from the doll to put in her hair to replace the ones that were taken.

Right then, I felt a crack on the back of my head. As I fell forward, Maude Annie hit me in the face so that my head swung back and hit the glass window of Hill's. The sound seemed so loud, I thought for sure the glass had broken. For days afterwards, my foster mother beat me and said the meanest things to me. The real trauma from it, though, was when we got to the summer house and my foster father, his brothers, and all my cousins were laughing at the news footage of the brutality toward the marchers. I heard them say, "Those damn black birds got what they had coming!"

I hid in my bed under the covers and tried not to hear them. I knew they were wrong. Mama Blanca and those I loved from my childhood were black and spoke French and treated me well. All I could think was, *What did they do wrong? What did that little girl do wrong to have her ribbons taken from her? The police only come when you've done something wrong, right? Did I do something wrong?* I just couldn't understand.

After this, I never spoke French again as a child. It was a child's distorted thinking, of course, but as I would witness my foster family lynch and kill African American people, I became more and more scared that they would find and kill Mama Blanca and maybe figure out that I needed to be killed, too. I began to believe

I could protect her and myself by hiding and burying my identity and memories. (I found out as an adult that while I was living with the Fosters, the KKK *had* boarded Mama Blanca up in her own house and burned it down.)

To add to my fear, when my foster father used to sexually abuse me, he would threaten me into keeping my mouth shut about it by reminding me I wasn't really white. He meant that the same things I witnessed happening to others could very well happen to me. I was given more and more reasons to hide myself. Ultimately, though, these experiences led me to pursue work in human rights with the United Nations. The reasons I hid as a child motivated me later to really fight back as an adult.

It was on this day, Bloody Friday, that I first saw someone else using singing to survive abuse. I wasn't alone in my abuse, it was happening everywhere, and these people had joined together to fight back against the system of abuse through a hymn of peace. The marchers were united through their suffering by linking their arms together and singing "We Shall Overcome" in the face of their abusers. And when they fell, they fell together. They were not alone. Their power came from risking their lives together to fight for their rights. Their voices rose above their abusers, and I realized the power in surviving and that it could be done with music.

10

My First Guitar

At age 12, I had begun working as a maid at my cousin's wife's house. I'd go every Saturday and clean the entire house. After I spent a year doing that, she wanted to give me a raise from $10 to $12 a day. Since every penny went to my foster mother, I begged her to not let my foster mother know about the raise. For a year, I saved that extra $2.

Everyone in my little town waited for the Christmas coupon flyers from Western Auto Hardware Store to buy the family Christmas presents—especially toys. I had seen a guitar in the store for so long, and I wanted this sunburst box guitar. I was ready to buy my first guitar to keep as my very own. My half-sister had the piano (even though she didn't care for music), and I needed to be able to make my own music. I went into the store and laid my coupon and money on the counter only to find out that my hands were not big enough to play the guitar. It broke my heart!

The store owner, Mr. Watson, said, "Well, I have a little guitar that didn't sell last year. I don't know how good of shape it's in since it's been in storage."

I told him to bring it out. I was determined to have a guitar.

When he came out, he said, "Now, this new one is $74, and this little one is $86. But it has been in storage for a year, and I just don't want to have to store it anymore. If you'll take it home, I'll give it to you for $76 with tax."

I only had $74.

He said, "Well, what Uncle Sam don't know won't hurt him, will it? I do believe it *is* $74."

I took it home and my foster mother discovered it soon after. She beat me in the head with the guitar, and then dragged me and the guitar back down to the Western Auto. She told the shop owner that I had stolen the guitar.

He replied, "Miss Foster, this child gave me money for that guitar, she didn't steal it."

"Well, she stole the money from me, then, and she's going to get it from me when we get home." And I did. She dragged me home with the guitar and beat me for days. Then, she made me wrap the guitar up and give it to my half-sister for Christmas. My half-sister couldn't care less about it, though, and she kept it under her bed.

When everyone was out of the house, I would sneak into her room and play the guitar. Well, one day I was caught with it. My foster mother hit me with it and then put it up in the attic where the rats lived. I had a phobia of rats because she would threaten to put me up in the attic to be rat food. To this day I am terrified of even the smallest mouse. It borders on a phobia.

When I graduated early at 17 years old in 1974, I was pushed out of foster care. I had been seeing a man named Donald who was eight years older than I was, so we became engaged. Before I left my foster home, Donald brought an empty guitar case to the house, and he got my guitar from the attic so we could take it with us. Leaving my foster home with my first guitar and the man I was going to marry felt like a new beginning, one in which my childhood was over and my life was really starting.

PART IV

Life Before Multiple Sclerosis

"God is Everywhere"
By Carolana Callaway and Mark Cawley
God is everywhere (right here, right now)
God is everywhere (right here, right now)
He's in every word we say
When we bow our heads and pray
God is everywhere (right here, right now)
God is everywhere (right here, right now)
Just as long as you believe
God is everywhere!

My marriage to Donald was not what I expected, but I had three beautiful daughters with him, and I will always be grateful for that. It's widely known that abuse stays within the body long after it is done. I think after so many years of horrific abuse from my foster family, I came to expect it as I became a woman. It was all I knew. The beginning of my relationship with Donald was okay. We both wanted to do missions work. We both loved the church and Jesus. We wanted to travel and see the world and do good works. Our similarities ended there, though. I loved to work and have a deep purpose in my career, and Donald liked to do the bare minimum. I was passionate and outgoing, and he was dark and brooding. I wanted to treat everyone with respect and love, and he was manipulative and distrustful.

As I built my identity parallel to Donald by getting a doctorate in Latin American Anthropology, beginning a career in journalism, and reconnecting with my past, I grew beyond our marriage. I learned that the things you learn from a broken relationship help you to heal in ways you never knew you needed.

The beauty of the horrors I had been through is that I survived them. With my face toward the sky and a song in my heart, I not only survived—I thrived. In this section, you'll see that ability to thrive in various forms. All along the way, music helped me to reconcile my past and find the ability to move toward a future I hadn't seen for myself. Without music, I wonder now whether my identity could have survived my trying times. My broken heart has repeatedly healed thanks to music. I learned to love again thanks to music. And without MS, I might not ever have begun to make music, my life's most rewarding career.

Reconnection in Venezuela

Reconnecting with my father was a very "God" thing. Donald and I were Southern Baptist missionaries, and we were scheduled to go to a seminary in Wake Forest, North Carolina, to then go to Nigeria. Before we left, though, we were told there had been an error in the paperwork at the Foreign Admission Board and someone else was sent instead, under Donald's credentials. They told us we had three choices for other options: South Korea, Barbados, or Venezuela. Barbados was an associate missionary position, and I wouldn't settle for anything less than a full-time career missionary placement.

I remember thinking, *Venezuela is so dirty*. I have no idea where that thought came from, but I wonder if I subconsciously associated the place with trauma from my past (the loss of parents and identity). Donald didn't want to go to South Korea, though, so Venezuela was our choice.

Once I got used to living in Venezuela in our gated neighborhood, I would take the kids to school and run errands on my own. Over time, I started seeing familiar faces. It was starting to feel like a home. Strange things started to happen, though. For instance, I had a beautiful mandolin that needed some repairs, and when I went to pick it up, not only was the repair paid for but the artistic decorations were also restored. I tried to argue with the man, but he wouldn't take my money. He said, "It's been paid in full, with a tip!" Confused, I left and went about my day.

Some time later, I went to the bodega near my kids' school where I would often go and get arepas, little cornmeal patties with cheese and butter. It was soul food for me. One morning, I turned from the cashier, and a man I recognized from outside the school was behind me. I was a little frightened.

He asked in a formal British accent, "Would you have a couple of minutes for me to get coffee with you?"

My instinct was to say no. Men there were very flirtatious. There was even a common phrase, "Take care of your wife or I will."

When I looked into his eyes, though, my soul felt a stir of shock. There was something there that I recognized beyond just a familiar face. I said, "Well, my car is parked in a no-parking zone."

"I'll have your car moved for you."

"No way, you aren't stealing my car!"

He smiled and said, "I won't be stealing your car. I could buy you other cars, anyway."

He then set a picture down on the table. It was a photo of a little girl in a yellow dress holding a doll. I'd never seen the photo before, but I had an odd feeling about it. Something about it made me think it was a photo of myself.

"Where did you get this picture?" I asked.

He said, "I didn't 'get' it from anyone. I took that photo. If you'll just have coffee with me, I can explain everything to you."

Against my better judgment, I gave my keys to a security guard who was with him. I was in shock, but I still couldn't quite trust this strange man. I said, "Let's sit by the window so people can see us." The bodega was tiny and we squeezed in around a small corner table.

As we sat down, he said, "You have no idea who I am do you?"

There was something so familiar about him, but I shook my head.

"Before I tell you who I am, I want to say that I don't want anything from you, I don't need anything from you. I just want to tell you who I am."

I nodded vaguely.

The waiter brought our coffees and the man held his cup toward me and said, "Let the duets begin."

I stared at him. "Papi. You're Papi." Questions flooded my brain. Why was he here in Venezuela, in my little town of Los Teques? Why was he approaching me now instead of when I really needed him as a child? I began to cry and I don't know what came over me other than a wave of emotions.

I jumped up and slammed my fist on the table and said, "How dare you come into my life right now, when I spent my entire childhood watching the roadway, sure you'd come back for me. And when you didn't, I just wanted you dead." I walked out of the bodega.

He followed me out and said, "I deserve every word you just said, but there's so much more you haven't been told. I was threatened to not come and see you. But I saw you in the music store, and I felt like it was time to try and reconnect finally."

I couldn't listen to him. I was blinded by emotion, so I left him there.

It took a long time for me to realize that music had bridged our broken relationship. If he hadn't seen me going into the music store, he might not have had the strength to try and repair our relationship. Music connected and healed us, even though I fought it out of my own deep-set fears.

Happiness in Venezuela

Over the next several months, Papi and I saw each other many times. I learned that he was a senior diplomat in Venezuela and was living in Caracas, the large city near our tiny town of Los Teques. He would drive to meet me, in secret at first because I wasn't sure how to explain him to my family and I was still so angry with him. I wish I had done more soul searching and less rebellion during that first year of reconnecting with Papi. I was so confused, but it doesn't excuse my behavior. No matter what I said, though, he always forgave me. I would give anything to redo that one year of my life. I couldn't see that he was sick. He was probably dying even then, and I couldn't let myself see it through my anger. I argued with him and said mean things. I demanded a DNA test to prove he was my father.

He said, "I will gladly do that, but I think you know we don't need it."

I'd been told that Momma's husband Charles was my father, and I had been forced to create that truth in my brain.

Papi showed me boxes full of checkbooks and check receipts from the child support he had sent for years. We stopped counting when we got to $80,000. All of them were endorsed by Maude Annie. I had remembered envelopes coming in the mail with my name on them, and Maude Annie would snatch them up.

I think Maude Annie had been stringing Papi along. He paid in the hopes of having visitation rights, but he didn't have rights as a foreigner. So even when he realized he wouldn't be able to see me, he kept paying, hoping they'd take a little better care of me. He knew those checks were all that kept me alive. He was afraid not to send the checks because I could have been treated even worse.

Over time I realized our similarities and could see the familial resemblance, but it took me years to allow the pre-foster care flashbacks. The first I really let come to me was the one of my little white shoes on top of big black shoes. I was out walking one day and was listening to Zydeco dance music used for Cajun waltz, and I had the sudden memory of being lifted into the air and swirled around and around to a fiddle waltz. My yellow, frilly party dress whirled around and flew up over my face. Then, suddenly, my Papi's face appeared. Sweat dripped from his hair, his ears, his neck, and each drop of sweat tickled my cheeks. I could almost hear the chatter around us, the happiness playing with the music. My head was on his shoulder, my face pressed against his sweaty silk shirt. The smell. It was wonderful.

I was stopped in the middle of the sidewalk as these memories flooded over me. After this flashback, I cried for days. I actually remembered him, and it was because I remembered seeing those feet.

When I talked about it with Papi, he filled in the details. This was when we lived in Ocean Springs, and my dad worked as a consulate in Mobile, Alabama. My Aunt Tibby was in medical school, and my mom's music career was taking off. We had parties where friends would stay at our house and the party would continue over breakfast. It was just a really good time in our life. This information felt familiar, but I was still distrusting of him and still so angry for having felt abandoned by him in my childhood. He had protected me as a small child. I waited for several years for him to come and rescue me from the hell of my life with the Foster's. I watched down the long winding driveway. When I came home from school, I would often see a strange car, and I just knew it was my Papi. But he didn't come. I grew to hate him for not coming for me.

When I finally realized Papi was who he said he was and I was flooded with memories I'd suppressed of my childhood before the Fosters, I went to Papi's house and threw myself in his arms crying.

He hugged me tight and said, "I never stopped loving you. They knew I was a fool for you, but I was afraid if I stopped sending the money, they would retaliate against you. I knew they were KKK and capable of anything, and I couldn't imagine what would happen to you."

I became that little kid again. I was home!

The context behind my childhood finally began to come together because I had found my true family. I was filled with the guilty dread of realizing how I'd treated Papi the previous year. He was so gracious, though, and was just glad to have his daughter back in his life. He gave me a drawing he had done of what he thought I would look like a couple years after I was taken away. He'd just needed to see me. That is a father's love for a daughter. I felt loved again, life made sense again, and I felt safe maybe for the first time. That is, until the exile of 1988.

13

Homeland Lost

In the early 1980s, Venezuela began a descent into a political and economic crisis that lasted two decades. In 1988, my husband was still a missionary, and I had become a journalist in addition to my mission work. As a press representative, even after a long day and staying up until 2 am to get an issue to print, I felt like the most blessed person in the world because I loved what I did. The political situation was becoming more volatile, though, and journalism was a dangerous occupation. As much as Papi tried to fight the violence and injustices, the strength of the insurgents was becoming too great for him to deal with on his own. His power as a senior diplomat could not fully protect us.

Without warning, we were summoned for interrogations in Caracas, an hour and a half from our home up in the Andes mountains. For the next couple of months, I had to take my whole family with me every 72 hours to Caracas where we would stay in an interrogation room for 24 hours at a time. We were put in the room with nothing at all.

Over and over my daughters and I sang together, "He's got the whole world in his hands." I'd hold them in my arms and rock them like little babies.

> **"Mommy's Lullaby"**
> *By My Mommy and Me*
> I loved you then
> I love you now
> And I'll love you
> When life pulls us apart.
> Each night I'll come
> In your dreams
> I'll come and sing
> To heal our broken hearts.

My children had nothing to play with, though, and they were frightened by all the noises and sights. To distract them from the screams and the blood on the door's window, I took my beautiful handmade eyelet handkerchief out of my pocket. I ripped a piece of fabric from my slip and tied it around the handkerchief to make a head, and I formed some semblance of a doll for my daughters to love. Here we were, one day living a normal life and the next day tearing my clothes to make a doll for my daughters.

Every time we would return home from the interrogation, our house was torn apart. I still don't know what exactly they were looking for.

Finally, after eight weeks of interrogations, some men came and told us to pack one small bag of essentials. We had 48 hours to leave. Then, they came in the middle of the night and set our house aflame. We made it out of the house in time with our small carry-on suitcase of essentials, but we just had to watch our home burn before going to the airport.

For the first time in my life I doubted God because I literally had blisters on my knees from pleading with him. My dad was a powerful man, and I couldn't understand why he wasn't making it stop. I had to deal with that anger with Papi. I didn't understand at the time that Papi wanted me out of the country to protect us, and he was allowing them to exile me.

When we got to the airport, they took the suitcase and handed me two diapers, and we were escorted onto the plane. We arrived in Miami with no credentials, no identification, nothing. We were strip-searched and spent hours in customs. Some family friends flew to Miami with luggage for us so we could have *something* to start a new life in the states.

My life felt surreal. I simply didn't know who I was anymore. I had finished my doctoral studies, was starting my journalism career, and was a press representative of the Southern Baptist Convention as a career missionary. My husband and I had three beautiful children and lived in a beautiful Venezuelan home. And then, suddenly, it was all gone. We had to start over.

My husband wanted to go do mission work in Africa because he couldn't deal with the pressure and shock of everything that had happened to us. I wanted to start over in the US, though. He became a part-time migrant missionary preaching to the immigrants who came to work for the Vidalia Onion Company in Glennville, Georgia. When it became clear to the Migrant Ministry Board that Donald seemed resistant to getting an additional job, one of the directors made a call and set me up with a teaching job. Suddenly, I was teaching the following Monday. Nobody had asked me what I wanted. I had a doctorate and was now forced to go back to school to receive my teacher's certificate while teaching full-time. I loved the children, but teaching was not my passion, and it was so difficult to leave the job I loved: journalism. I was scared my writing career had just died!

After a year of teaching, I became a Migrant Education Coordinator. I began working with the migrant workers' children, and I watched the lice run up and down their arms. Part of my job was to make sure the children and pregnant women weren't out in the fields and that they adhered to child labor laws. I had to examine home conditions and make sure they had medical care.

I never dreamed that all those farm owners were abusing those children. I didn't know until a little boy came to school vomiting. It was the first time I heard of the Mexican slang term "agua caliente," which literally translates to "hot water." I asked him what had happened, and he told me a man put his hot water in his mouth. As the story began to unfold and we did mouth swabs, we found the problem was widespread. The parents knew, but what were they going to do? In their culture, they might sell a child to get money for their family. Without documents, they don't have rights.

We had to get the Federal Immigration and Naturalization Service involved. The cases lasted years. There were hours of films of the abuse that needed reviewed to be used for evidence. Hundreds of tapes, hundreds of kids. I couldn't tell my family what was happening, and to see people I knew going into those trailers made me crazy. Some people were prosecuted, but nobody with money, of course.

I felt like the legal system had failed me. I'd been exiled from Venezuela, and now I was feeling morally exiled from the States. I knew God had the little tiny babies in his hands, the whole world in his hands, but I realized God's hands were moved by people. Our actions simulate God's hands, and I wanted to hold the whole world in my hands and make it better. This desire is what motivated me to go into law five years later and led to my work as a Human Rights Investigator in DC for the United Nations.

14

A Broken Marriage

Venezuela was the catalyst to the end of my first marriage. We'd always had problems, but something deep broke in him and between us, and we divorced in early 1992. Before we divorced, though, I was diagnosed with cervical cancer, which was found at a routine gynecologist visit. My doctor sent a sample to biopsy, but he knew what it was. It may have been in the early stages, but it was cancer. The shock of this and the stress of being in a bad marriage for so long caused me to break down in front of my doctor. I told him about the details of our very challenging relationship. Donald had explosive anger that took its toll on our family and on me.

Donald didn't seem to want me to be "smart." He made sure I knew that—time and time again. I even had to go to church knowing we had a rough marriage. My stomach was just sick about it. I tried to cover up and hide our bad relationship from my children because they had gone through enough in their short lives already. In addition to cancer, I had this bad marriage on my hands too.

My surgery was scheduled right before Christmas 1991. I didn't tell my children about the cancer or the surgery because I thought they had already been through too much. I bought the children presents, prepared a feast, and left directions on the counter. Then, I went to a friend's house for the next few weeks while I recovered from the surgery.

After recovering from the surgery, I gathered my strength, returned to our home, and began the process of getting legally divorced. Once my husband and I divorced, I unfortunately had to live in the same house. Every day was scary, not knowing what to expect from him.

I had met my second husband Brian at this point; we'd met through mutual friends and hit it off immediately while listening and dancing to music, and before long we were married and I was able to take the children away with me.

Christy's Dance Home

My daughter Christy and I are too much alike. Our minds are evil together, and the things we laugh about would embarrass the devil! We'll spend hours on the phone yacking and cutting up, but it wasn't always this way. Our relationship broke one Christmas, and it took almost a decade to mend, and only thanks to the survival power of music.

Christmas was always a happy time for my children, and I loved singing Christmas carols with them. But Christmas of 1991 changed my relationship with my daughter Christy and emotionally scarred her for life. That was the year I was diagnosed with cervical cancer, and my doctor had told me to leave my marriage or else find another oncologist. A teacher friend of mine, Nancy, offered her home and time in another town nearby. She and my other friends saw me through what turned out to be a two-year ordeal with recurrent bouts of cervical cancer.

Because it was a few days before Christmas when I left for Nancy's, I prepared the girls' Christmas presents and froze a special dinner before leaving for the hospital for surgery. I left Donald a list of where to find dinner and the girls' surprise presents. In retrospect, I should have told the girls about my cancer, but at the time I didn't want to spoil their Christmas. That proved to be a horrible mistake that led to a horrible Christmas for my girls, especially for Christy, who was 16 at the time. I found out years later that while her father lay in bed depressed on Christmas morning, Christy had to fix breakfast for the younger girls, Bethany and Lindsay, while fighting back tears because she had seen the Christmas tree was bare.

After breakfast, the younger girls ran into the living room to open their presents. But there were no presents under the tree. When they asked Donald, his only answer was that Momma was the one who always put Christmas together, and she had left and taken all his money so there'd be no Christmas. What happened to their Christmas presents and frozen dinner? Several years later I found out that he had disposed of everything—he even got rid of the family dog in his anger and grief! To this day, I cry when I think about it.

I left the hospital on Christmas Eve and before going back to Nancy's, I felt a strange urge to buy more presents for my girls. I went to the mall and seemed to keep running into things on sale that I had already bought them, but I felt compelled to buy them again. I felt like I must have been acting irrational, but to this day I believe God was warning me about their lost Christmas.

Late on Christmas Day, the girls came to Nancy's, and I got to give them presents. We had a wonderful time together. I felt distant from Christy, though. I felt like I had let her down. It seemed to me like all the adults in her life had let her down—on Christmas of all days! I was supposed to be the "Momma" and I had left her. The better I tried to make our lives, the further apart I felt from her.

In 1992, her resentment grew deeper when I met, and later married, Brian. He was such a kind and caring man. My two younger girls, Lindsay and Bethany, instantly bonded with him. However, Christy saw him through the scars of her life. She refused to give him a chance.

Less than six months into our marriage, Christy decided to move in with her father instead of living with Brian and me. The distance between Alabama and Georgia made the gulf between us grow even wider. I think she felt the need to take care of Donald and his loneliness. Where there had once been little communication, there now was no communication. I didn't know what had happened, and she thought I just didn't care. Every Christmas without her brought back the pain and heartache of Christmas 1991. Each year that passed made the sadness stronger, and I would spend time alone, missing her. I wept to God to bring home my lost child.

At 2 am on Christmas of 1998, eight years later when Christy was 24 years old, there came an earth-shaking pound on the door of my Northern Virginia house. At that hour, door-pounding could only mean something tragic had happened. I ran down the spiral staircase to the front door, but stopped because I felt a pause of fear run through my body. The pounding continued, and I finally pulled the door open to find my own Christmas miracle standing outside. There stood Christy!

Sobbing, she fell into my arms and said, "Mommy, I heard the song you used to sing to me, and I knew I had to hear you sing it again!" She told me about going to a Christmas choral concert at the University of Montevallo. The choir sang Sidney Carter's "Lord of the Dance." She was struck with the memory of me singing that song to her many times before the Christmas that broke us. She heard my voice singing it to her and she burst into tears, rushed to her car, and drove all night Christmas Eve from Montevallo, Alabama, to Springfield, Virginia. Her swollen eyes told me she had cried most of the 800-mile, 11-hour trip to come spend Christmas with me and find our song of reconciliation. We sang it over and over again during her time with me. Once again, music had led to survival. An estranged mother and daughter's relationship survived—thanks to the power of music!

16

Burning Feet

Soon after I married Brian and we were living in Monroe County, Georgia, I woke up in horror one night because I felt like I could smell burning flesh. Little did I know this was a flashback to a childhood memory. As a child I had witnessed the KKK burning people, but I didn't know why I could smell that terrible smell now. I suddenly felt horrible pain in my feet.

My aunt Margaret was still alive at the time, and I asked her, "Did something happen to my feet?" She wouldn't answer me, though.

A couple weeks later there was a military ball held in Biloxi near Ocean Springs. I went to the ball with Brian. Everywhere I looked I felt like I was having deja vu. I felt like I was in a strange dream and I went to the beach to clear my head.

While I was sitting in the sand, a memory came to me clear as day. I remembered being in the waves, Mama Blanca holding me. My feet were bandaged, and she was letting the waves soak off the bandages. She was a natural healer and believed in the healing power of salt water and the trace minerals floating in it. Somehow I knew this memory was connected to the sense memory of the smell of burning flesh.

The last time I saw my Papi, when I was much older, I asked him, "Papi, did my feet ever get hurt when I was a kid? I remember how I sort of walked on the sides of my feet. I also remember smelling burning flesh and Mama Blanca washing my feet in the ocean, but what actually happened?"

He said, "I had always prayed you wouldn't remember this." He told me I started walking at a very young age, at about nine months old, and I was running when I was just a year. My mom had convinced him to let her take me to meet my brothers and sisters. Against her better judgment, she had left the house and left me in Charles's care when he was drunk.

Charles wanted to hurt me. There was a floor furnace with a big grid grate on it. He picked me up and forced me to stand on the furnace. That was the smell of burning flesh I'd remembered. I had a flash of a memory of screaming against the searing pain while strong hands held my feet down on the grate.

Papi told me that just hours after I'd been taken to Charles's, my Papi had had a bad feeling and drove all night with Aunt Tibby. I don't know where it would have all ended if Papi had not come to get me. He told me he regretted not calling the police, but all he could think was to rescue his child.

Tibby attempted to give me medical attention in the car, but Papi said I screamed all the way back to New Orleans and was still screaming two days later. He said I was inconsolable. I was emotionally and physically traumatized. The doctor said I wouldn't walk again; my soles would never heal enough for me to walk. Mama Blanca knew differently and she worked on my feet for a year to heal them. She made a salve from a mixture of East Indian spices like curry, turmeric, and saffron mixed with Vicks Vapor Rub. She gently massaged my burns with the rub to heal the wounds and prevent the joints and bones from locking from disuse. She would sing to me and rub my feet in the salt water until the sticky, bloody bandages came off, and then she would repeat the process.

Papi said that I didn't try to walk again until I was two years old. It took so long for my feet to heal, and I wanted to dance so badly but would say softly, "Oh, I can't."

He told me that on my third birthday I pulled his sleeve and said, "Dancy feet." He put me on his shoes, and we danced together. It was then he knew I would be all right.

I grew up feeling so self-conscious of my feet and I was spanked for not walking "right." Your body has memories, even when the memory is suppressed mentally. As a kid I would get mosquito bites on my feet because the skin wasn't thick enough. I'd get big sores on my feet and I would relive the pain of that night without quite knowing the memory that was causing it.

Decades later in 1993, after marrying Brian, I showed him a dancing jump without warming up and I landed wrong. I broke my foot in two places. I was too proud to go to the doctor, though, and after awhile, I realized there was a growth forming on the foot. I finally went in for the surgery. There was a tumor. The nerves had wrapped around the bone and underneath a tumor that had grown into a hook shape and was suffocating the bones, joints, and blood flow. The procedure was supposed to take 20 minutes, but it ended up lasting over two hours.

After the procedure, the doctor asked me, "When were your feet badly burned?"

It caught me off guard. "As a small child. I had an accident and they were burned."

He nodded. "I could tell. I didn't have much skin to work with."

There's a reason they are called the "soles" of your feet. Feet ground you both physically and psychologically. I believe part of your soul lives in your feet, which is why Jesus washed his disciples' feet. Part of my treatment for my MS today is to soak my feet in water mixed with volcano ash and salt in order to remove the toxins my body accumulates during the day. It's a daily purifying of my soles.

My feet have represented my soul in that they've been beaten, burned, cut, and lost, but they always heal. My soul has suffered, but it always heals, too, thanks to love and music.

Papi Creates Survival Keys

Early in 1960, Papi took an assignment working with the Embassies of Costa Rica and Panama. It was the last time we traveled overseas as a family. Papi had many interactions with Panama's de facto ruler, Manuel Noriega. In 1992, Papi was in the group that testified against Noriega during his trials in Atlanta. He had information about the drug activity between Noriega and the FARC (the Colombian armed guerrilla group), to which I was never privy.

Before he testified, though, I remember Papi told me that he used to always know when the UN was going to transfer him. He said, "The first step is divine discontent. There's just that ill-fitting feeling, not that you're mad at anybody but that you don't feel you fit anymore, and you're not plugged in like you were. Then, I'd start getting those little road signs."

I asked, "What do you mean by 'road signs'?"

"Well, if I was going to be sent to India, someone may ask me to lunch at an Indian restaurant, or I'd find incense from India or someone I used to know from India would pop back up. There are always road signs, you just have to keep your eyes open to them. It's not like one thing happens, like a Damascus Road experience. It's not going to knock you down blind. It's little things, a show on TV, a smell of masti rice in the market. Discontent is God's way of turning your radar on so you can pick up the messages around you."

He told me that his divine road signs were leading him to the Noriega trial being held in Atlanta. He knew he would likely be assassinated after testifying against the still-influential Noriega. I begged him not to testify, because it put his life in danger. He said he had to testify because he had to make the world better for his three granddaughters.

Papi said, "If I don't, that's another drug lord walking the streets that could hurt my grandbabies. This is what I do to keep democracy alive in Latin America."

He testified in Atlanta and took the embassy plane back to Miami, but we didn't hear anything from him for a year. We now think the FARC had the pilot killed and flew Papi to Colombia.

Tibby told me later, "I don't think they did anything to him that could have been worse than what he experienced at Auschwitz." She also suspected that Papi may have been intentional in testifying because his health was getting worse and he was becoming debilitated. He knew the power of those he testified against, and Tibby thought he knew it was a suicidal move. Papi had also developed MS, but I can't say for sure when it manifested. Papi and I were separated for so long, I'm not sure what he was going through in my foster care years.

The first thing I knew of Papi as an adult was when I had my first child when I was 17 years old. Donald stayed in the waiting room during her birth. Later, he told me a man with a cane, who looked exactly like me, was in the waiting room and would listen in when a nurse came out to give the status. The man never approached Donald, though. I thought it strange but let it go.

Five years later, when Bethany was born, the same man was present in the waiting room. Donald told me the man's limp had gotten significantly worse, and the man asked after me. Donald didn't know who he was and prevented the strange man from going back to see me. When Lindsey was born, almost five years after Bethany, Papi was there again. At this point, he was having difficulty walking altogether. We were living in Venezuela at the time, but we had rushed back to the US for Lindsey's birth. This was before Papi had approached me in Venezuela.

After some time passed since I'd last heard from Papi after he testified against Noriega, I started getting mail with blood on it. Not totally understanding who it was from but knowing it had to do with my inability to get in touch with Papi, I just thought, "How did they find me in this tiny Georgia town?"

About a year after his disappearance, my cousin Lucy contacted me and said there was a photo in a Colombian newspaper that looked like it could be Papi. She sent me the photo and I couldn't believe it. It didn't look like him. We learned later that he had 14 broken bones in his face and was barely recognizable because of it. The news story included a warning that implied that this was what could happen to anyone, even a Venezuelan dignitary, who spoke out against the Colombian powers that be. Needless to say, I was devastated.

When I lived in DC, years after I learned of Papi's death, I was at the Colombian embassy giving tours as part of my job. A janitor came up to me and handed me a bundle of papers. He walked away immediately, and I never found out who he was. I have no idea why he saved those documents or how they got to me. What he handed me was Papi's journals during his prison time in Colombia. I can hardly read them. When I try, I can only read a few pages at a time. Afterwards, I cry for days. It's like all Papi's journals—they're sacred. Some documents are meant to be savored before being shared.

In the first few pages, he wrote about how he took his own blood from the torture to create a piano on the wall. The bars from the small window cast a shadow on the wall, which looked like the black keys on the major scale. He counted the bricks around the shadows and drew the black keys with blood so he could still play and hear music in his head. He would try to remember the sound of each key so he wouldn't lose his sanity, which a lot of prisoners did. This was a place where you were lucky to have something to sleep on, lucky to have a rat for company. The isolation would drive you crazy. They would also move the prisoners periodically to different rooms. Papi wrote about how he would have to remake a new piano on the wall every time he was moved.

These were his survival keys. He'd wanted and needed music so badly to survive that he used his own blood to draw it. Without his music, he might not have survived that year of captivity.

He would "play" the keys by humming the notes from memory. He talks in his journals about how he had to figure out playing the C and E key together, and the quarter chord he missed one day but would get right the next day. It almost became like a composition and musical theory book. He also talked about the guards, young boys with machetes, who would ask him to teach them to play on the piano. In return, the boys would bring him a pencil and paper to write, or a small morsel of food that would help him stay alive. They loved to listen to him play by voicing the notes he had drawn on the wall. He also knew that if he kept playing his music, there would be days that would go by without a beating. There was a desperation for music. It saddens me to know how much he must have yearned for a piano, but I'm proud of how strong he was for enduring what he did. He wasn't going to pace himself into insanity.

I don't know what triggered the final beating that brought about his death, but it's amazing he survived as long as he did.

There's no mistake that I used music to survive. I came from a long line of people on both sides of my family who survived through the power of music.

I spent a long time missing him, wishing him to return. But honestly, it would have broken his heart to see me like this, to see my children show signs of the same medical deterioration I'm experiencing. In some ways, I'm glad Papi didn't have to see me so debilitated by MS. As much as he struggled with the sickness himself, I know it would have broken his heart to see his baby with the same sickness. And it would have been even more devastating to see his granddaughters and great-grandchildren show the early signs of MS. So even though I would've preferred to have many more years with Papi, I'm proud of how he left this world. He wanted to leave the world better than he found it for his family's sake. And no matter his conditions or situations, he always found a way to play his music.

18

The Diagnosis That Changed My Life

A couple years after we got married, Brian and I moved to DC, and I began law school and was hired by the UN as a Human Rights Investigator. My first assignment with the UN was a trip to Bolivia in 1999 as a field reporter, and my daughter Lindsey came and spent the summer with me. My work was challenging but rewarding because it held so much purpose.

One particular mission to Colombia exemplifies the type of work I did. The FARC in Colombia had told a village to go into a church to keep safe. As soon as they were inside, the FARC bombed the church and trapped everyone inside, leaving any survivors to die. We were sent in as glorified body counters almost two weeks after it happened. The stench was burned into my nostrils and traumatized me to the point that I can't smell things the way I used to. When we were going through the church we heard whimpering. We found a six-year-old boy, pale as death, who had survived by living under the bodies for two weeks. He thought he was dead, but he didn't understand why it didn't hurt to be dead.

He couldn't even identify his parents' bodies because the dead's skin was falling off at that point. Years later, when he was in his 20s, I heard a report that he still wasn't sure he was alive.

My last mission with the UN was to Ghana in 2006. I loved Ghana so much so that I later adopted two children in Ghana who were HIV positive. I couldn't bring them back to the states, but I hired the children's grandparents, a pastor and his wife, to raise them. In 2016, the oldest of the two graduated medical school.

On this trip in 2006, though, my assistant Gabriel and I were posted in Ghana for a project in a small country in the ear of Africa called Sierra Leone. We were working to stop the horrors against women, including the gang raping of young girls and women's breasts being sliced off with machetes. One meeting I attended had breasts lining the sidewalk in front of the building as a warning to us. I had dealt with so much pain, loss, and abuse in my own life that I vowed not to let this behavior continue to happen to women.

One day on this trip, I was extremely fatigued and could not get out of bed to go to a meeting. I was startled to find that my left leg was entirely numb. I couldn't even feel the sheets on it. In retrospect, this was one of the first clear signs of the onset of MS. Gabriel went to the meeting in my place, and en route he was shot by a sniper. They were so skilled they shot him in the jugular, above the bullet proof vest and below the helmet, and he died almost instantly. I had worked with Gabriel for eight years at this point, and he ended up taking a bullet clearly intended for me. He was an only child and his wife had just had a baby. I'm still close with his parents in Quebec. They refer to me as a daughter, and they gave me his helmet.

I never traveled again for the UN. I was put on medical leave, and after countless doctor's visits, I was finally diagnosed with MS in 2007 and given the prognosis of three to five years left to live. My file with the UN was pulled and made inactive.

PART V

Living with Multiple Sclerosis

"Blessed by the Master's Hands"
By Carolana Callaway
Tiny can be mighty,
When blessed by the Master's hands.
All things are multiplied,
From his hands we are supplied.
Little really matters,
Though we can't understand.
Tiny can be mighty,
When blessed by the Master's hands.
. . .
When you plead, "Lord, I'm not able!"
Trust his hands to hold you stable.

I was misdiagnosed many times before finally being correctly diagnosed with MS in 2007. While living in DC, I was diagnosed with a failure-to-adapt "conversion illness." My seizures didn't show on the EKG so I was also told that I was faking it, even though there were lesions on my frontal lobe showing the damage. It was more convenient to not diagnose me. I finally got a correct diagnosis in Atlanta in 2007, and when my doctor told me I could have three to five years left to live, I was distraught. I cried for months thinking about how my time was cut so short.

Within a year of the diagnosis, I began to write songs as a form of therapy for my soul. I went to workshops and was surprised others wanted to sing and buy my music. Then, I began getting awards and recognition for my songs. Just when I thought my life was over, God stepped in and had me living in the music world, something I'd never done before in my career. It was as if the prognosis gave me extra energy to get done what I could before the disease could take me.

Then, I began writing about what was happening in my MS treatments, and I realized writing about living with MS was so therapeutic! I don't feel in control of the disease taking over my body and mind, but I can control writing about it. If I think of writing about it as though I'm writing a song, the words come more easily to me. If I can communicate the horrors of the disease through metaphor and symbolism, I can get a reprieve from the actual pain.

This section will give examples of how I moved from associating MS with Multiple Sclerosis to taking MS to mean "Mighty Songwriter." These are snapshots of what it's like to live with this disease daily. Life weaves in and out of these events as my condition continues to spiral downward. I wake up every day and just try it one more time. Some days I get it, and some days I don't. But I know my writing has helped me and others, so it's all I'll do till I'm done!

19

Becoming Silent and Still

Since infancy, singing has been as natural to me as breathing. But in 2008, my MS cast a deep shadow of silence over my passion for singing.

I moved with Brian back to the Washington, DC area. I'd hoped to have access to better medical care, but that was not the case. My condition continued to deteriorate. Each new doctor had another medication to try to stop my muscle-ripping, full-body spasms. Each time I was rushed to the hospital with another full-body spasm (sometimes called "Stiff Person Syndrome"), a new drug was added to my already overdosed levels. Within a few months, I was on a cocktail of anticonvulsants that exceeded the recommended level by over 25 percent. As the dosages gradually increased, so did the side effect of speech problems. It became increasingly more difficult for me to form even a simple sentence. Embarrassed by my speech, I preferred not to speak at all. But I still enjoyed listening to gospel music and humming along.

Then, the dreadful day came when I opened my mouth to sing, and suddenly I realized—I could no longer sing!

My soul burst open with a waterfall of tears from almost five years of frustration with my MS. I cried, and cried, and cried. I looked up at the clock and realized that I had been crying for almost 12 hours. I cried until my soul lay dry without another tear. In my head I pleaded with God, "Take anything from me, but do not take my ability to sing!" Then, my heart shouted to God, "First you take my words. Now you take my song? What kind of God are you?" And then my soul screamed to God, "I have worked so hard to overcome a childhood scarred by severe abuse, and this is how you reward me? If this is how you care, then stop caring about me!"

The only answer I got was: "Be still!"

I was stunned for a moment after hearing the answer. Then, my humor kicked in, and I thought to myself, *Like I have a choice?*

God's wisdom had placed me where being still was the only ability that remained of my former strength. Those 12 hours of tears somehow healed my heart that night, and I sat in silence until dawn the next morning. In total silence—I was still. I had emptied my soul. I had finally learned how to "Be Still." In that night of being still, I had no other option but to listen. As dawn broke, I realized that I had imposed my stubborn will on God by insisting to always do things my way. My abusive childhood had left me with a stubborn will to survive and an inability to trust others. But now I would have to trust God. Only he knew his plans for the rest of my life. I had not only been broken to stillness; I had also been broken to silence.

That stillness brought me the gift of learning about my heavenly Father more intimately. Learning of him in this new way transformed the very foundation of my world. He was no longer the occasional God I took off the shelf during a crisis. He was increasingly becoming my only source of strength, even helping me to breathe.

Under his direction, the first thing I knew I must do was to gradually wean off the mood-altering anti-seizure medications. I felt fearful of this because the meds helped lessen the severity of the painful night-spasms. The night-spasms would cause the muscles in my neck to tighten, and I would often choke or lose my breath. Each night, with the accuracy of an alarm clock, the spasms awoke me at 3 am. I prayed through my fears. I constantly craved the beauty I felt during those "Be Still" moments with my heavenly Father. My passion to feel those moments far outweighed my fear of the spasms. I was determined not to go back on the medications. I could find marginal relief in sitting in an old swivel rocking chair that I bought on sale at the Goodwill.

The rocking chair's repetitive motion soon brought out an instinctive need to remember the hymns my great-grandmother had sung to me as a young child. At first, I could only hear them in my mind's ear, but those memories soothed my aching body. For months, I would spend the early morning hours rocking to the rhythm of the hymns in my memories. My list of favorites began to grow: "Just As I Am," "Oh, How I Love Jesus," "He's Got the Whole World In His Hands," and so on. If I couldn't remember the verses, I just made up the words. Each new song I remembered brought hope that one day I would speak and sing again.

I was faithful to praise God in my pain, and he was faithful to heal my soul and body. Praise God! One day when I was silently singing in my heart, I was startled to hear myself humming—not on pitch or in tune but in a new form of joyful noise. The sound was primitive yet filled with praise. What mattered was that I could sing! A musical sound had made its way up from my heart, past my vocal cords, and out of my mouth! All the education I had achieved was no competition for the accomplishment I felt in that pre-dawn morning. After so many years of seeking and serving my mind, I had finally found my heart! I didn't have to go out and seek my heart's song. I just needed to Be Still and let God give me the song my heart needed most.

The God of Appearing Normal

In the Bible, God says, "You shall have no other gods before me" (Exod. 20:3) as a warning against idolatry, but I am sure that was written before Multiple Sclerosis (MS) was discovered. After meeting MS officially in 2007, I came to know the god of appearing normal, an idol that tempted me to love it more than God. This is still a struggle for me. Appearing normal has become more than a passion for me. It has become my false god. Others often applaud my behavior by saying, "You look good! You look like you aren't sick!" (Aka: You look "normal"!) Their words send me back to bowing to the god of appearing normal.

I work hard at bowing before the god of appearing normal. Bedtime is a perfect example. I hate going to bed because resting is so much work. An oxygen condenser has to be set at three liters, a bi-pap machine must have chemical-free water, Amrix must be taken two hours before Melatonin, Clonazepam must be taken just as I go to bed (so it will numb pain and last all night), a pillow must be under my limp left arm (to promote circulation), and the list goes on.

Worse than the process of going to bed is the getting out of bed. It exhausts me with pain. I wake up before dawn with bone crushing, labor-like pains in my lower back. During the night, my brain misfires and sends an overload of signals to my back muscles. Those faulty signals are stored in the lower part of my spinal cord. The pain from those trapped signals wake me with blood-curdling screams daily. Until my brain finds my legs, I am paralyzed within that pain. While trapped in pain, I often wonder if one morning I will wake up and my brain will not be able to find my legs ever again.

Yet in spite of such inner fears, several hours later, I am up, dressed fully, and my face is made up. Why? Because appearing normal is my own form of denial of my MS. In my mind, if I worship the god of appearing normal enough, maybe my disabling Multiple Sclerosis will just go away. Maybe it will just fade away while I'm exhausting myself trying to be normal.

Behind the false curtain of "appearing normal," I am literally struggling with getting out of bed. I feel like my feet are sunk in buckets of cement and I have to walk with that extra weight all day, every day.

In addition to body pains and muscle issues, my mind is scrambled by the MS and I spend my day trying to stop the constant flipping of channels in my head. Random thoughts flash through my brain so regularly that my MS has robbed me of the ability to organize my day without constantly checking a written "what comes next" list.

• The God of Appearing Normal •

I made it out of bed, check. I got dressed, check. I took my meds, combed my hair, ate breakfast, brushed my teeth, check-check-check-check. What's next? Time for my morning Bible reading, but thanks to the brain fog of MS I have no clue where I last put my Bible. By now, the stress of checking my list every few minutes only to be met with this roadblock makes me so frustrated that I feel hot tears run down my cheeks. Like a helpless child, I collapse into my overstuffed rocking chair and do what I did as a child: I rock and I sing "Just As I Am," "Amazing Grace," "His Eye Is On The Sparrow." On and on I go, singing the verses that come to me and filling in my own words for the verses I have forgotten. My tired mind and heart float back to the deep Creole voice of Mama Blanca. She sang to me with such passion that I often think she must have known that someday I'd need those songs. She didn't choose lullabies. She chose hymns of comfort and wisdom as she rocked and hummed to me.

Suddenly, my bitter tears of frustration with MS melt into tears of gratitude to my loving God who created me. My tears remind me that if he created me, then he will keep me no matter what happens. Submission to him means accepting that I am in the vessel he chooses to use me in. Whether I'm weakened by MS or a striking runway model, the vessel he puts me in is totally his business. God has a daily plan for me, and instead I spend my time putting energy toward the god of appearing normal. If he needs me to have MS to fulfill his purpose for me, then I must accept my MS and stop fighting so hard to deny it. Maybe I am meant to encourage my medical team, or maybe there is someone I will never know who needs to see me being gracefully weak and struggling. Either way, letting him give me courage during painful, helpless moments allows his power to be seen through me. My helplessness allows room for his helpfulness to shine! When someone looks at me, I don't want them to see a woman suffering with MS but rather a woman able to get up and walk, thanks to the power of her loving God!

21

Just Shy of Suicide

I used to wake up with Christmas morning excitement for each new day. Even during my hardest times working with the UN, I woke up optimistic and energized to fulfill my purpose. Even during such a dark childhood, music and church helped give me a purpose that woke me up ready to face whatever difficulty came my way.

Now, I wake up with pain so severe that I feel just shy of suicide.

The first back-arching pain is the worst one of the day. It feels as though someone is stabbing the small of my back with a knife. No matter how exhausted I am, when the pain medications wear off, my body is awake. I'd like to roll over to relieve the pain, but my MS brain is not awake enough to move my limbs. So I am paralyzed in pain until my brain can connect to my body. Every morning I must lie there with my back muscles in such tight spasms that they've caused hairline fractures in my spinal vertebrae.

Suspended in labor-like pain, I wait until my MS-fogged brain slowly remembers how to move my body. It's as though my mind and my body do not belong to the same person. Daily, they have to get reacquainted with each other. Meanwhile, the palms of my hands and soles of my feet feel like acid has been thrown on them. My hands are drawn up in a hardened fist. My feet are locked in a sickled arch. I cannot open the spasmodic locks of my hands or feet. My fingernail beds turn blue from the lack of circulation during the night.

Each morning begins the same. I lie there in tears from the pain, often begging God to let it all end. I've just awoken, yet my body already feels an end-of-day fatigue. One thing I have learned about pain is that it takes courage to live with it and not die from it. The pain of Progressive MS can be both exhausting and depressing. Sadly, I have lost several MS friends to suicide, yet I understand their reasons.

My left side is very weak from the Progressive MS, so I have to wait until my right side is ready to compensate to get out of bed. I have carefully placed my bed close to the door frame between my bedroom and bathroom so that once I am standing, I can balance myself on the door frame. Standing up brings another round of bone-breaking pain as the pain from my lower back radiates down to the muscles in the back of my legs. I hug the door frame and brace myself against the waves of pain shooting down my legs.

Once I am steady on my feet, I attempt the three steps from the doorway to the commode. I pay a very high price for those first three steps each morning. Those first painful steps leave me faint and dizzy from the horrific pain. I sit on the commode and lay my exhausted head over on the vanity. I am drained of all energy. Through my sobs, I ask God, "Why don't you just take me? I can't do this again today! What purpose can there be in such suffering?"

God waits patiently for me to finish my pity party. Afterwards, he reminds me that he has allowed me to wake up and breathe for another day. He gives me this day because he still has a purpose for me to live it. No matter how the day begins, it still has purpose. Each day is a new surrender to his plan and not my plan. I see my body as deformed and broken, but it is still God's vessel. He created it. So he gets to decide how he will form my body to best use it on this earth. Each day, he allows me to breathe is another day that he has "re-created" for me.

When I touch a piano key or hear the scratch of my pen across paper, I am reminded that as meager as my efforts may be, God has still given me talent and expects me to use it for his purpose. Knowing that my life still has meaning and purpose takes me from just shy of suicide to feeling joyfully alive.

My Humble Gift

"Enjoy the Christmas lights this year: you may not be able to see them next year—if there is a next year. Your brain lesions have doubled in size in just six months. We have exhausted all medications to slow down the growth of your lesions. Your prognosis is very uncertain. All I can say is lean into your music and your songwriting—they produce endorphins and they are better medicine than anything I can give you in a bottle. Your music is your lifeline. Literally!"

After telling me this with tears in her eyes, my neurologist, Dr. Gretchen Campbell, turned and walked out of the room. It was Christmas 2014, and my MS was getting worse. Over the previous few years, she and I had faced one defeat after another with my Progressive Multiple Sclerosis. Before this appointment, I'd felt stronger and hopeful that my MS was perhaps going into remission and that I might have a short rest from the downward health spiral. So her words shocked me to my very deepest core.

As I walked down the long corridor to the parking deck, I kept repeating to myself: "Do not cry, you have to get home." I knew if I cried the first tear, a floodgate of tears would open and I might not be able to stop my weeping. I needed to cry but I also had to drive home alone in the congestion of Nashville's afternoon rush hour. Plus, I had to get yet another prescription for my muscle spasms filled. I sat silently numbed at the Kroger Pharmacy while the friendly staff attempted to carry on a bright, cheerful conversation with me. I didn't hear a thing they said.

It was dark when I finally arrived home. Physical fatigue and blurred vision plagued me, but I had been successful in not shedding a single tear. I was so alone in the darkness of my garage. I was so empty in the numbness of my heart. How was I to enjoy Christmas if I could neither feel the joy nor see the lights? Now that I was safely home, I could cry—but no tears would come!

It was Christmas Eve before Brian and I were able to travel from Nashville to our family home near LaGrange, Georgia. About an hour into the trip, my back and body spasms began and continued throughout the next six hours of driving. About an hour from LaGrange, we stopped at a truck stop so I could try to walk and relieve the spasms. Walking inside the store, I suddenly realized that all I could see were outlines of figures and shapes. I could not focus or see details. In a panic I grabbed Brian's arm and helplessly begged to be led to the restroom. In the safety of the restroom, I tried to calm down. I thought to myself that this must be rock bottom. It couldn't get worse.

Unfortunately, it did. On Christmas morning I awoke with a sharp pain in my right eye. I couldn't even open it without screaming. Brian rushed me to the ER where we would spend our Christmas Day. Both eyes were strained and fatigued from the MS, but

• My Humble Gift •

I had torn the cornea of my right eye. The ER doctor patched the right eye and advised me to avoid as much light as possible for a few days. I couldn't even cry out my frustrations because the tears would only make my eyes hurt more. How could I celebrate Christmas surrounded by the darkness of such horrific pain? *This* was rock bottom.

Worst of all, how was I to finish my memoir without my vision? God had opened doors for me to be trained and befriended by the very best Christian writers such as Gloria Gaither, Dottie Rambo and her daughter Reba Rambo McEntire, and Susan C. Smith. All were repeated Dove Award Winners with nationally admired wisdom. If I could even write again, how could anything I write do honor to their wonderful instruction? For the first time, I felt I did not have a gift worth giving to the baby Jesus at Christmas.

Heartbroken back at home in Nashville, I sat alone in my library surrounded by all the books I had once read. Through the silence, I heard the angelic voice of my six-year-old granddaughter, Dalayla, singing "Little Drummer Boy." In her own paraphrase of the lyrics she sang: "My gift is poor for him, but it is my best for him."

When we do not hear God, he speaks through the voice of a child! How did that poor little drummer boy feel standing beside the elegant gifts of the rich wise men? After all, they were not just wise men, they were also wealthy rulers who held supreme titles from their kings. I felt humbled by my little granddaughter's song and felt as though I were a little drummer who was just doing her best for God and Jesus.

Several months later, my neurologist smiled at me, full of her own hope for me, and said, "New chemotherapy has just been approved for advanced MS and as experimental treatment for rheumatoid arthritis. Now you have new hope—you can start living again!"

After so much talk of my death, the very thought of "life" brought grateful tears to my eyes. Maybe I would see Christmas again!

For years I had been given treatments of white blood cell replacement therapy once a month. This therapy leaves me feeling like I have a bone-breaking flu, and if the seizure medication isn't strong enough the transfusion will cause days of seizures. When the therapy begins, a hot flash of fire burns through my spinal cord and for the next six to eight hours I have to sit still and endure.

Then, the dosage frequency was increased to every three weeks. At any given infusion, my body could suddenly reject the donor white cells—then what? There were no other possible treatments!

The question of "then what?" has covered my life like a large black robe of fear. Even when I am writing and flying high on my pen, that dark death robe covers my heart. God's grace has met my faith and together we have soared way above my MS, in spite of the dark robe.

But finally, a new chemotherapy gave me the chance to shed that dark death robe of fear and have new hope! New hope means a renewal of life. I started "1cc" of chemotherapy once a week in a shot form. The chemo kills autoimmune cells just like it does cancer cells. It doesn't treat pain, but it slows down the deterioration of my joints and helps keep things from getting worse.

In the 24 hours after my doctor told me about the new drug's FDA approval, I wanted everything around me changed and given new life. I dragged my beloved desk over to the sunlit dormer window. It barely fit, but wow, what a view! From my desk I could see out over the pond to the pastures, everything glazed in a whole new shade of wonderful. The sight of those pastures truly restored my soul with new hope and life, and I felt like God had granted yet another gift to his little drummer girl.

23

Not to My Child!

"We've tried everything, now we need to operate on your back," explained my spinal specialist, Dr. Klekemp of Vanderbilt Orthopedics, in late 2014. He continued, "There are risks—especially with your Multiple Sclerosis. There is a 15 to 20 percent chance that you could be paralyzed. But I'm going with the 80 percent chance that we can help with some of your pain."

I sighed. "Well, Dr. Klekemp, we both know that MS will eventually get my legs. The left one is numb and drags already. The right hurts all the time. Truth is, the pain is so horrible that I'll risk anything. Crippled is better than in pain!"

In spite of my pain, the earliest date for surgery would be four weeks away. But Dr. Klekemp's calendar is like the parking lot of a really popular restaurant: they are both full because they are both great. So with my narcotic pain medicine in hand, I headed home to wait out the four weeks. I was glad for a little extra time to get ready. Each of the eight doctors on my MS Team would have to be visited to approve the operation. But four weeks is a long time for the fear of the outcome to set in too. But I knew at Vanderbilt I had the best doctors in the country. Each time I felt fear, I thanked God for bringing me to Nashville—close to them and close to him. My heavenly Father gave me peace and my heart was ready.

Two days later, all my thankfulness and peacefulness was shattered by a phone call from Dr. Klekemp. A closer look at my MRI showed what could be a spur or piece of bone that could be pressing into my spinal cord or a major nerve or both. This had been the reason my right leg suddenly started cramping and caused my entire spinal cord to arch! He said: "MRIs show us so much, but they have limits. I'll feel better when I see for myself what's actually going on." Surgery would need to happen ASAP.

Within a few hours, I received word from Williamson Medical Center that one of Dr. Klekemp's patients had canceled their surgery date. The surgical nurse said, "No one ever cancels a surgery date with Dr. Klekemp! He's that good. You have been given a rare gift! Can you be ready by Wednesday?"

I was in shock. "Wow! Well, absolutely!"

My waiting time shrank from a few weeks down to a few days. Instead of visiting my MS team of doctors, Dr. Klekemp's office faxed out letters explaining the urgency. By the next morning, all the team doctors had faxed back approvals. Amazing!

It seemed like a miracle, and maybe some would call it that. My next thought was, "Is my spinal problem so serious that all these doctors are jumping around to get me into surgery?" All of the rush froze me in fear. I couldn't speak or write a word. I stopped, dropped, and prayed! I felt the protection of my heavenly Father wrap around me like a warm blanket of love. It was his protection of my spine that was rushing everything and getting it in place. Only he could really see inside my spinal cord. He arranged time and ordered the surgery to protect it. Like all loving parents, he used everything in his power to protect his child. His love melted all my frozen fears. Now, I could trust that he had everything in his perfect order.

The day of surgery finally came. I arrived at Williamson Medical Center for my 7:30 am surgery. Fear crept back when the admissions nurse told me, "You may have a long wait. Dr. Klekemp wants to take you last—just in case there's an unexpected problem." Around noon, the surgery began. I drifted off to sleep with my head on my heavenly Father's broad shoulders. I felt as safe as a trusting toddler. He had this in his mighty hands.

Later, Dr. Klekemp explained the results of the surgery. As expected, a piece of bone spur had to be removed from the lining of my spinal cord. It took three stitches to repair the damage the spur had done to the lining. He also found several lumbar vertebrae almost completely compressed flat. Those were drilled out and fused together correctly to allow room for my spinal cord to expand. That required another ten stitches. I had a lot of post-op pain, but I knew my spinal cord had been saved! One hard speed bump in the road could have pushed that fragment into my spinal cord and permanently injured it. One of those damaged vertebrae could have shifted when I stood up or sat down, and that could have cut off circulation to my spinal cord. The "could haves" are endless.

But I put my faith in God's hands, and my heavenly Father looked down and said, "No, not to my child!"

24

The Guilt of Survival

On May 27, 2015, I got the news that a dear family friend Randy had died from MS complications. I heard this while I was getting an IV blood infusion (IVIG). My access port had thrown a clot and the 12-hour blood infusion had to be given in a tiny vein in my wrist. I screamed with pain as my body began to reject the donor blood. When the IVIG fluids reached my spinal cord, it provoked a migraine that made me feel like I was dying. I wanted to cry for Randy's passing, yet I felt jealous that she would not have to face another day of this kind of pain.

In the previous 18 months, I've lost five friends to Multiple Sclerosis. Some had less severe cases than mine and some had more severe, but almost all of them were younger than I. The number one reason people die from MS is organ failure. The brain sends nerve impulses, but they misfire or don't reach the intended destination. The organ dies even though the brain is trying to reach it.

While I am grateful for any extra time here on earth, I often feel guilty for getting somewhat better and hanging on. I oscillate between a feeling of gratitude for improvements and a feeling of anger at the injustice of MS taking someone so much younger than I am.

I often grieve the person I used to be before MS. My brain is in a constant state of chaos. I feel stupid when I can't get my fingers to remember simple guitar chords. My legs are getting weaker so now I wear a leg brace that starts at my foot and runs all the way to my hip. It's heavy and it often takes more energy than I can muster to drag it onto my leg and attach it. I can't seem to escape the unrelenting pain from my brain misfiring signals to my muscles. One day I may be twisted like a human pretzel from the muscle spasms of MS, and no matter how hard my brain tells my limbs to loosen and relax, the signal will misfire and I'll suffer the shock of paralyzing pain. It's like I am still in my body but someone else controls it like a puppeteer. In those moments, I understand the high suicide rate among patients with Progressive MS.

My Christian morals will not allow me to consider suicide as a means to escape the pain. I also know that committing suicide would scar the legacy I want to leave to my children and grandchildren. Many researchers believe that the tendency to be suicidal is hereditary. I don't want my three daughters always looking back over their shoulders for the suicide monster to appear. My suicide would cast a dark shadow over their lives and maybe the lives of their children. Knowing the effect my suicide would have on their lives adds another layer of guilt to my survival.

The Guilt of Survival

I'm not sure exactly when I began feeling this survivor's guilt, but I can go weeks without feeling the guilt of survival, and I can even convince myself I don't have it at all. Then, when I hear of another MS death, I think to myself, *But for the grace of God that could have been me!* I fall into a deep, dark mental hole and realize I have not escaped, nor cured, my survivor's guilt. The guilt alone is like another sickness I carry with me all the time.

I feel guilty for being alive, for surviving another day no matter how painful it was. Watching the others die makes me feel guilty for complaining about my chronic pain, mental fog and forgetfulness, or disabling fatigue. I remember my friend Randy and how she bravely weathered 17 years in a nursing home due to MS complications. Who am I to complain? I still live at home. I can have a nurse come and give me my monthly IVIG at home. I can still type and communicate via social media. I'm usually able to write down some words in my journal or in this book or scribble a few lines of a song. I'm able to do a little work on a craft project. The thing I am most proud of is that I'm still able to refuse my wheelchair. Each day God gives me strength to do these things in spite of my chronic pain and unrelenting fatigue.

Like a soldier fighting on the front lines of a battle whose buddies are being killed left and right, at any moment he may be shot down too but he's always hoping to make it to the end of his tour of duty so he can go home. The difference with MS is there is no end to the tour of duty. The battle of MS is a lifelong war that will gradually scar you until death is a welcomed end during a battle. I will be fighting it until the moment I die.

Sometimes Progressive MS is like waiting for your turn to die. Each time a member of the group is gone, I feel a whole new round of guilt for still being alive. In some ways it feels like I'm starting to grieve my own death, because a little piece of my soul dies with each of them.

Glass Houses

A habit I've acquired with my MS is building glass houses. One glass house is constructed on the wish for healing. I'm always trying to convince myself that I'm getting better, that I'm kicking this MS and one day it will just go away. That's a very fragile house, and as time goes on and my body continues to slowly break down, I see the house is crumbling.

Another glass house is one made of the hope that I can handle anything on my own. I go to a Multiple Sclerosis support group and feel the deepest guilt of all those in attendance. Everyone in the group has an "assistive device" such as a cane, walker, or wheelchair. Against my doctor's advice, I walk into the building alone. Even though I'm weak and in pain, somehow my self-righteous refusal to use an assistive device proves to myself that I am getting better, that I am not as "sick" as the other members.

My stubbornness to walk alone is a fragile, glass house of hope I have built for myself. It often crashes, like last year when I had a severe fall, but I quickly rebuild and move on. The walkers, canes, leg braces, and wheelchairs I've gotten per my doctor's advice are crammed as deep inside a closet as they will fit. I want any reminders of my MS as far out of sight as possible. If I can avoid needing the prescribed and recommended "assistance devices," then I can avoid MS altogether.

It works! At least until suddenly I notice a new numb spot on a limb that refuses to bend or I fall and can't get up. A fall from MS is no "Med-Alert" gimmick or joke. When MS strikes your body with a fall, there is usually no getting up alone. I feel even more guilty because I had the medical devices to avoid the fall, but my pride wouldn't allow me to use them. My fall was my own fault.

Another glass house I've built is one of believing that the aesthetic changes of my body are temporary. I don't want to believe that this almost 270-pound body I see in the mirror is really mine. It's so different from what I've been used to seeing the majority of my life. Most days I lounge around in dirty, week-old pajamas with no makeup and my hair put up so I don't have to comb it. Who am I anymore?

The change in my body started when I was diagnosed with colon cancer in 2014. When the doctors completed the surgery and removed what needed to be removed, they warned me that I may struggle with insulin and pancreatic functions. They said my body could start processing food as sugars and I needed to eat more protein.

Recently, I was tested, and sure enough my pancreas was not accurately processing the food I eat. I've gained a lot of weight over the last couple years, and I'm just now starting to lose it thanks to a new medication. Although every blood infusion adds dextrose and my body swells up again, so I feel like I have to start over every month.

Almost any physical activity drains me, so I'm already fighting an uphill battle. Even something as seemingly simple as playing my piano has changed for me. I am ashamed of my clumsy hands as they try to play and fail, and it's like reliving that same feeling of missing the steps while dancing. It can sometimes paralyze me in fear of trying new things. I've now lived so long in a state of inactivity due to my sickness and pain that it took a lot of courage to try something active.

I had considered swimming, but the doctors advised against it due to my balance issues. In September 2018, I decided to take matters into my own hands. I got some goggles and went to the nearby recreation center. Although I was a bit fearful, I swam a couple laps. I was so proud of myself! It felt so good to move again with a seemingly functional body. I miss dancing, but it felt good to find something to give me that same sort of high of doing something I love.

It's a lot of work to face the fears of the new person the MS has made me into, but I'm working on breaking through that glass ceiling. It took me too long to realize that while my time on earth is limited, if I'm not doing the things I love, then the time isn't meaningful at all.

PART VI

Reconciliations

"Pain Beyond Your Prayers"
By Carolana Callaway
In the midnight hour of her heart's nightmare,
Jesus whispers in her ear.
These same hands that made you,
Will get you through this too.
I'm holding a bottle to catch,
Your every tear.
Cause that's how much I care,
When you got pain,
Pain beyond your prayers.

Reconciliation is very important to me. Sometimes it's more important to reconcile with loss than hold on to a dream of being reconciled with that person. For instance, it's not a possibility to reconcile my relationships with my half-brothers and half-sisters. Two have died, and I can no longer hope for that family reunion that would bring us all together as one family. I can't control wanting my family reconciled any more than I can control my terminal MS.

I also can't fully reconcile with my previous self, the self before this body broke down into one I no longer recognize. The person I once knew is gone, and I am now and forever will be the Carolana with terminal, malignant MS. It's hard to hold all these memories of someone I see as a different person, a person strong enough to survive both childhood and domestic trauma, while holding a job working for human rights; a person capable enough to leave a bad husband and finally start life over again. I am now a person living with debilitating MS who tries to accept the mood swings and personality changes that come from MS. I terrify myself.

I will try to reconcile what I can, though, before I sing myself to heaven. I owe it to myself. I've lived an amazing life. From living and working in Venezuela with three young children, to working for the UN and being diagnosed with MS, to becoming a grandmother and a songwriter in Nashville, there are so many experiences that have brought meaning to my life. Every challenging experience has made me who I am, and I'm truly grateful to God for all the gifts he has given me. I hope to pass along this book as a gift to both my future generations and any reader needing encouragement and hope. Reconcile what you can while you are here, and you'll have no regrets when you're singing your way to heaven.

We'll Fly Away

As my own health grew weaker, I felt the need to find my biological mother. In 2008 I began to intensify my search for her. Over the years, I had heard bits and pieces about her drug addiction. All I could gather was that she was probably in a nursing home for former drug addicts. I just had to find the right place and nursing home!

I followed every lead and clue that I thought would lead me to Momma, and I even went so far as to hire a private investigator. But because my mom was in a nursing home, he could not violate her right to patient privacy. I kept trying every nursing home in the greater Birmingham area—over and over again.

In 2015, my daughter, Bethany, joined me in the search. Through sheer determination, she managed to get the name of the facility where Momma was living. Bethany immediately shot me a text with the information. I spent the next three days repeatedly calling the number, always being blocked by the HIPAA Act.

But on the third day, God sent me an angel in the form of a nurse. It was no mistake that her name was actually "Angel." She recognized my voice from the many times I had called and was told no. Once again, I tearfully pleaded, " Ma'am, I really need an angel. Won't you please help me find my mother?"

She replied in a friendly laugh: "Guess that's why my mommy named me Angel."

My heart jumped up to my throat when she said, "Child I know you really want to talk to your mother. I've taken most of your calls asking for information. Yes, Ms. Virginia Barrow lives here in our facility. Fact is, I'm her caretaker nurse. She's real lonely, and needs someone to visit her. Truth is, she needs you as much as you seem to need her."

Ms. Virginia Barrow lives here! Those were the most beautiful words I could have heard. Those five words were more important than holding a winning lottery ticket because I had finally found my Momma!

Nurse Angel went to get my mom to the phone. But she was still asleep, so Angel asked me to leave my number, and she would have my mom return my call.

Waiting for her call was like waiting for a baby to be born. The time just gets longer—not shorter. Two hours passed, and I was sure she just didn't want to talk to me. The phone finally rang. It was Angel.

"I'm sorry," Angel explained, "But Ms. Barrow says she doesn't have a daughter living in Nashville. Nor does she have a daughter named Cheryl."

After decades of missing my mother, how could she not know me? How could Momma not know that I was calling out to her with the desperation of the same small child I was the last time I saw her? Suddenly, I felt that all my searching was the biggest mistake of my life. All my childhood, I had been told stories of how she abandoned me, and now I was being left again?

I could hear Momma's voice in the background as she yelled, "I told you I do not have a daughter named Cheryl—I told you that!"

Hoping she could hear me, I yelled into the phone, "Mommy, I'm your Carolana—not Cheryl—I'm your Carolana—your little Carolana Margaret!" I wanted to jump through the telephone and show her that it was really me.

Then, I heard a joyful shout that sounded like an amen corner of a tent revival meeting. Momma cried out, "Oh! Carolana. Thank you, Jesus! Oh! It's my sweet Angel Girl! Of course she'd be in Nashville—she was my singing angel!"

Nurse Angel burst out a laugh, "Oh my goodness! Child, I thought you said your name was Cheryl—not Carol! Ms. Virginia is gonna hit me with this phone if I don't give it to her."

I choked on my own words. I was five years old again. My mind was flooded with the memories of Momma singing to me. I suddenly realized why Nashville seemed so much like home. It was the place Momma told me about, and she sang me songs about it.

Back then I did promise her, with all my heart, that I would go to "Das-ville" and sing and make new songs one day.

After that first phone call, I spent the next 24 hours wondering what I would say to her when we first saw each other. But we didn't need words. Our eyes met, and we spoke the language of tears. Our arms hugged so close that our hearts felt like one heart beating.

I knew her arms from the minute I fell into them. I was finally home! After decades of searching, I had found her. We wept and tried to hold each other tighter and tighter. Like every other child, I had never forgotten the feeling of my Momma's hugs—even after all these decades of searching for her.

It took us over an hour to stop crying and hugging. Nurse Angel stood over us with an ear-to-ear smile. Her smile was so wide I could almost count her teeth.

Momma looked up at her and finally spoke, "This is my only baby that would stand next to me while I was cooking and beg, 'Sing, Mommy, sing!' She'd pull my apron so hard it would fall off, and I would have to sit down and sing with her 'cause she might've pulled my dress off too. Of all my six babies, this Angel Girl was the only one that would sit still long enough for me to sing to her. And as soon as she could talk, she could sing most of the words to our songs!"

We heard singing coming from the dining hall. It was time for the Sunday service to start. Momma's eyes sparkled with excitement.

She grabbed my arm and said, "Come on, Angel Girl! Sunday is the only time I get to sing anymore. Hurry, let's don't miss the singing!"

She giggled as she said, "Push Mommy's old wheelchair fast now. It's my turn to hear my Angel Girl sing to her Mommy. I can't wait to hear you sing!"

She led me to her assigned table. We got seated just in time for the singing to start. By this point in my life, I dreaded singing. For months I'd had tightness in my throat that was thought to be from my MS spasms. I was afraid to sing at first. My voice had not been worked for months, and I felt like my singing voice was trapped inside my chest. I hated that feeling, yet I didn't want to disappoint Momma.

Then, the group began to sing the old, loved hymn "I'll Fly Away" (by Albert E. Brumley). As Momma tried to sing, she looked so weak and faint. She laid her head on my shoulder and whispered, "That song was your favorite lullaby. When you'd ask me to fly you to sleep at night, I knew you were very tired. I'd know that you wanted the fly away song." She went on to say, "Now, I am so tired, and I need you to sing to me, Angel Girl." She wrapped her arms around me and held me close, like when I was a small child. Now, Momma needed a lullaby. The last time I had seen my momma, we'd been singing together. She sang into my ear moments before we were separated.

I knew I had to try and sing for her even though I had done everything possible to awake my singing voice without success. I had tried professional voice coaching, speech therapy, and even endoscopic stretching of my esophagus. My voice had remained trapped for so long. But at her age and weakened health, I knew that I might not have another chance to sing for her, so I joined the church group singing.

It turned out that all my voice needed was to find Momma and hear her say: *"Angel Girl, sing with me."* As I sang, I felt like a bird had been released from my throat. That little bird was my love for singing! My voice—my little bird—had been trapped in the prison of grief from missing my Momma.

The problem with my voice was not in my throat—it was in my heart! When I sang, my heart heard Momma singing and grieved her deeply. Without my mother's voice, my heart had a hole in it. And without a full heart, my songbird could not be set fully free! All children need their mothers—regardless of their age or stage in life.

I knew Momma's age made her time short, and I knew my health could make my time short as well. But I had found the peace to know that we will soon both fly away—maybe together!

The Gift of Dementia

Before leaving from my first visit with Momma, she reclaimed a tradition that left me with a memory that has changed me forever. Just before I left, she reached inside her daygown pocket and handed me a tattered, crumpled piece of paper. She tearfully smiled and pleaded, "Sing it! You still know it! It's Momma's Lullaby—Song In Our Hearts."

> **"Song In Our Hearts"**
> *By My Mommy and Me*
> I loved you then,
> I love you now.
> I'll love you
> Till death we may part.
> Now and forever,
> We'll be together
> Joined by the song
> In our hearts!

With a tearful voice, I sang the last words I heard her sing to me, before I was snatched away from her. She shared with me that those words had changed a little over the years—mostly because she had given up on ever finding me. Due to her dementia, she only finished the chorus to the song. She had carried that same old crumpled paper all those years. She'd hoped to finish the verses, and that I would someday hear them on the radio and remember her. However, after losing me, her grief became so great that she never finished the song. Momma said she sang the chorus almost daily as a prayer for God to bring me back to her. She told me she wanted us to finish the song together.

As a Nashville songwriter, I have had many wonderful opportunities to co-write with great and gifted songwriters, but this was the one co-write my heart had craved all my life—it was a chance to co-write with Momma.

Nobody at the nursing home even knew Momma could sing or had any musical talent until I arrived on the scene. Afterwards, she began singing all the time. They also didn't know that she spoke French, but Momma immediately began speaking in French to me. She knew it was the language of my heart, and the nurses were surprised to hear us talk in perfect French together, especially because Momma had advanced dementia. It was like I was her little girl again because her mind had gone back to that place in time.

At other times, she would remember and tell me bits and pieces of her life over the decades that we had been apart.

After she had gone back to Charles, he forbade her from playing any and all music. He knew music empowered her, and he wanted to keep her entrapped in her depression. He was a truck driver, so when he was gone, she'd sometimes fall back into singing and humming. I have one memory of Charles coming home early and hearing her singing to me when I was maybe two years old. He beat her so badly, and as a little kid I felt like it was my fault.

Several years later, she would also lose custody of all her children due to a family dispute. Momma fell into a deep depression after losing her children and having been prevented from playing music. She began doing a lot of drugs just to cope with the day-to-day sorrow of her life. Even after finally leaving Charles for good, she couldn't cope. She had sacrificed her soul with her silent song. She married another man years later who encouraged her music, and she would occasionally sing in the gospel quartet every now and then. But the pieces of her soul that lived in music had all but died in the years of abuse and depression.

But now, because of her dementia, Momma had a chance to redo my early childhood years. We sang together and laughter filled her room and our hearts. Now she was the child, though, and it was my turn to brush her delicate hair like she had always done mine for me as a child. My daughter, Bethany, and I bought new earrings, lipstick, finger nail polish, and fancy purses for Momma. Bethany's daughter, Dalayla, adored dressing her newly found great-grandmother up in all the new diva, girly goods. We wanted her to look like the wonderful lady that we knew she still was inside.

Momma repaid our kindness with laughter. For example, on the Thanksgiving after our reconnection, we brought her to my daughter Bethany's house for Thanksgiving. Between Tuscaloosa and Birmingham a tornado hit, so we stopped the car on the side of the road to wait out the storm. Momma was scared out of her wits and leapt from the car, moving faster than we'd ever seen her move.

She raced to the driver's door in the rain and demanded, "I'm driving and getting us out of here!"

Anytime we took her on outings from the home and the GPS would tell us directions, my Momma would fight with it saying, "Who's this woman who won't shut up? She keeps interrupting my sentences! I know where I'm going!"

She always thought we were going to New Orleans, and she would ask if we were going to see my father, whom she called "Purty Boy."

Nine months after being reunited, on Easter Sunday, she whispered to me, "I'm goin' to see Purty Boy!" I knew that far away look in her eyes. "Angel Girl, can't you see your Papi smiling at you?" My adult self knew what seeing angels meant, but my inner child wanted to beg her not to see angels, yet! My child's heart was thrilled that I would finally have my Momma for our first Mother's Day, and I tried to distract her from the angels by showing her the matching dresses I'd bought us. She held her silk dress next to her cheek and rubbed away her tears of joy. She fell asleep hugging her new Mother's Day dress. I slipped away while she slept peacefully with a joyful smile on her face.

Halfway back to Nashville, a nurse called to say Momma had taken a sudden drop in blood pressure. She asked if I could return. The nurse explained, "We've never seen Ms. Virginia look and feel as good as she has when you are around." A few hours later that day, I arrived back at the nursing home. Momma could barely speak.

Momma's voice was weak as she whispered to me: "Finish our song, angel baby. People need to hear our heart song. And I will sing with you everyday from heaven."

I never got my first Mother's Day with Momma. She died a couple weeks before Mother's Day 2016. When I saw her for the final time, she looked so peaceful and had a slight smile on her face. She was under a purple blanket I had made her, and she looked so beautiful, just like I remembered her as a child. When they rolled her out of the room, the staff lined the hallways to pay their respects as she came by them. In the lobby, the staff told stories about her. Everyone loved her. We sang "I'll Fly Away," and I sang the words, "We'll Fly Away." My heart was lifted as I sang her to heaven!

From Fury to Forgiveness

Papi had two pianos, a small one and a large one. Aunt Tibby loved the little piano because she had smaller hands. She told about how she'd sit me at the piano, and we would play the keys or play pattycake. She's also who taught me to dance and to love dancing. She was my dance teacher and bought me my first pair of ballerina shoes, which I still have packed away with her dancing garb. She was a ballerina even during medical school because it was a way to relax. She had a beautiful voice and would sing with Momma, and they taught me to sing too. She lived with us because she was in school, so there was always someone around to walk the baby and sing to her.

Because of the unfortunate custody split, I lost Aunt Tibby when I lost Papi. I didn't reconnect with her until much later than I did with Papi. Once we reconnected, though, we connected like old best friends. We would make dolls together, and she would fill in details of my childhood and pass along mementos she'd kept all those years of separation. She and I spent hours talking, and she reminded me of all the French lullabies she'd taught me as a young child.

Just six months before Aunt Tibby's untimely death, I'd had to make the decision for my mother to enter into compassionate withdrawal. She had wanted a do not resuscitate. I'd had to sign those papers, and then less than a year later, I had to sign the papers to pull the plug on Aunt Tibby. During a riot instigated by terrorists in France, she was all but trampled, and shards of glass were imbedded along her entire body and several organs were crushed. She fought for her life for two weeks. Aunt Tibby had filled the void my mother had left when she died. What's more, I had talked with Aunt Tibby for several hours a night, most nights since my mother's passing, and now I had to let my other mother go.

Over time, my cousin Pierre, who handled Aunt Tibby's affairs, did some research on the names that were released as the terrorists during this particular attack, and he began to compare them to some of Aunt Tibby's documents. She was an in utero surgeon, which is a highly specialized job within obstetrics. Several times she went with Doctors Without Borders to deliver at-risk babies in the Middle East. She was a detailed note-taker and had kept her records on all the births she did with Doctors Without Borders. As Pierre went through her charts, he counted six names that directly matched those of men arrested for the terrorist attacks.

I was shocked. Aunt Tibby had brought these men into the world, and they had taken her out. Pierre found that she had even delivered one of these men's babies that very morning.

I suffered trying to reconcile this. For the first time in my life, I felt hate and I didn't know what to do with it. I finally had to tell

God to help me forgive them because I didn't believe I had the power to forgive them.

Just as music had taught me so much already in my life, it is what taught me forgiveness. I had a recurring dream of Aunt Tibby in her ballerina garb in a ditch, delivering babies one after another. The colors of the babies changed and flowed, and she sang as she worked, "All the children of the world, red, brown, yellow, black, and white, they are all precious in his sight."

She stood, covered in other women's blood, and held a baby in her arms. Suddenly her gown turned white and she said to me, "Think of them as the little children."

For months I sang the song over and over again until I finally could see these men as the little children they were. These terrorists were just as much God's children as I am. God raised Aunt Tibby out of the ditch, just as he raised me out of my past of abuse. She'd delivered these babies in the gutter, and she met her end in the gutter at their hands. It's doubtful they knew who suffered at their hands, and maybe had they known they would have thought twice before something that would lead to her being crushed underfoot. I think they lost an ability to see who they were hurting. They only saw a larger idea, not the humans around them.

Without that song, I could never have gotten past this. Even though I've now forgiven the terrorists who killed my Aunt Tibby, I still have the pain of that loss in my heart.

A Moral Dilemma

In early 2018, I'd gone two weeks of seeing a different doctor every day, and every single one of them said there was nothing they could do about my constant pain. At this point, I was begrudgingly using a walker full-time, and we were discussing wheelchair options. I was having five to six seizures a night. My seizures are very cruel because I'm awake the whole time. I wish I had the kind that you pass out and don't know it's happening. When you're awake and it's happening, you become so detached that it's like looking at the world through a big glass wall with the knowledge that you could be stuck there forever.

When I got transfusions, I had to take tons of seizure medications because my body did not like the foreign blood. I was getting cups worth of blood every transfusion. The doctors were having to give me so much seizure medication that by the time the day was over I was barely conscious.

I had started having trouble swallowing. The doctors found a large bleed right where the esophagus joins to the stomach, and they clamped that section of the esophagus off to stop it. Then, after another month or so, I had another and they were able to stop it with some medication. But since non-steroid and anti-inflammatory medications can cause bleeding, I was taken off a lot of my medications, including Celebrex. The doctor kept me on the 21-day white blood cell transfusions. If they go one day past 21, my own system will start producing white blood cells that will attack my red blood cells.

When all this was happening, one of my doctors said, "I can't prescribe this, but have you considered cannabis oil?"

"Medical marijuana? I don't think I'm interested."

"No, no, that's not what I'm talking about. CBD oil is legal in the state of Tennessee, and you could buy it at any vapor shop. Yes, it's a product of medical marijuana, but there's little to no THC in it." He also said, "Do not let yourself be in pain. It's harmless to take CBD oil. Your body will take what you need, and what your body doesn't need will be disposed of just like vitamin C."

I had not heard of CBD oil. I had to come home and make a hard decision, and I was struck by so many emotions. This could really be the end. My doctors had said, "You can't take anything for pain or you could hemorrhage to death." What about my arthritis? What about my debilitating MS?

I became so afraid, and I sat in my sunroom and cried for hours. I've had several friends "check themselves out," as we say. *I'm not suicidal, but the pain from MS is maddening! But do I go into this dark underworld of vapor shops to purchase this stigmatized product that can't be on record? Am I pro-medical marijuana, or am I*

A Moral Dilemma

anti-medical marijuana? Is marijuana the same as cannabis, and what does that mean?

Thinking all of this over, I mentioned it to a sweet nurse friend of mine, a dear lady just as Appalachia as she can be (God love her!). She was on the phone immediately with her son to see if she could get me some "miracle" marijuana that night. Oh, I laughed so hard! I told her, "No, no, no! I don't want that!"

I'm a collector of predicaments it seems.

But, I have a God-given will to live.

When I took my first dosage, I woke up the next morning with an optimistic feeling. It was the first time in years I had slept all night without pain! For weeks, I slept through the night, and it felt glorious. My bodily pains dulled and my seizures stopped. I couldn't drive because of the mellowness, but it was worth getting to feel like I could live again!

The irony of all of this is that I went to Christian colleges, I was a virgin when I got married, and I'd never done drugs my whole entire life. And, now at my age, I'm willingly taking CBD oil. It's like acne and wrinkles in the same phase!

When I went back for a check-up and another endoscopy to check on the bleed spots, I told the doctor, "By the way, I need to add herbals to my medications because I started taking CBD oil."

My doctor said, "Well, I could tell there was an improvement! CBD is good medicine. It's a very good medicine, even if it's not going to be approved by the FDA."

When I got a recent transfusion, I started feeling the start of a seizure, feeling a little detached, and my nurse said, "Where's your CBD oil? Girl, are you out of your mind? This is the one day you better keep it handy!" I hurried and got a dropper and gave myself the half cc, and within twenty minutes, my body was calmed down.

At the point of writing this in the summer of 2018, I have taken CBD oil every day for two months. It does not now last me through the night, but I'm only taking a half dose and haven't stepped up to the full amount. I'm trying not to step up for psychological reasons. I want to know that if it gets really bad, I still have a next level to help.

CBD oil has helped me live. It's not reversing the damage done by MS, but I'm able to feel like myself again. I'm able to laugh again, and that's worth breaking the taboo!

30

Missing Chromosome: An Answer

Being chronically ill becomes a full-time job. In the back of my mind, it sometimes feels so surreal. Like, *What's wrong with me? Why can't I just have arthritis, not rheumatoid arthritis? Why can't I just have MS, not Marburghs MS?* It's like a perfect storm!

Recently, near the end of the summer in 2018, I got test results back from my doctors that show I have a mutated chromosome. Doctors know very little about this particular chromosome other than it is a C protein, a necessary component for a healthy immune system. It's a protein that fights rare diseases. A and B proteins fight off common illnesses, even measles and mumps. C proteins are like the body's "special forces": they create the immunities that tackle the rare, strange diseases. The medical world really doesn't know the full repercussions of missing that piece of the chromosome, but what's clear is that Mengele's experiments at Auschwitz did something that affected the children of his test subjects.

How do I know this? I'm fortunate enough to be a part of my godfather's research group. He is a geneticist who is studying the effects on the offspring of Mengele's researched twins. Since Papi was one of his subjects, I was admitted to the research group. The common thread for all the offspring of Mengele's subjects is that every single one of us has MS. Regarding the discovery of the broken chromosome, my godfather said, "I really don't know what he could have done to cause chromosome mutations in future generations. Mengele was a mad scientist, but he was also a genius."

My dad never sat down and said he was a Mengele twin. He was too traumatized by it. He told me the one story of his time at Auschwitz that led to my being named Carolana, and he referenced the horrible medical experiments, but he never said Mengele's name. I don't think he could. I only found out years after his death when Aunt Tibby told me. Tibby said she was not surprised he hadn't told me, though, because even when he lived in Venezuela and heard a rumor that Mengele was alive and doing experiments on children living in Brazil, he moved to the US. He was scared to death of Mengele, and Brazil was too close.

Does this mean Mengele succeeded in his deranged experiments? The suffering he inflicted on his test subjects, both during the experiments and afterwards, is now filtering down through the generations in the form of a broken chromosome.

My biggest fear is, did I pass this broken chromosome on to my daughters? They all have health issues and show signs of MS. Even more frightening, is this passed on to my grandchildren too? They've had tests done that have shown the early signs of possible future autoimmune diseases. Autoimmune diseases usually manifest in puberty, and my oldest grandchild is nearing that age. I'm afraid. I know it's not my guilt to carry because there's nothing I can do about any of this, but I carry it still.

I cry for my father's pain, for what he must have gone through. What did that evil man do to him? At the same time, my survivor's guilt comes back because I'm happy to have an answer to what is happening. I'm glad to know the cause of my own pain. I'm sad Papi went through so much pain, but it would crush him to see me suffer too, to see his grandchildren and great-grandchildren potentially suffer the consequences of his torturer.

This is just another area I have to reconcile: regardless of the cause or effect, nothing changes the fact that I must continue to do my best to survive my MS for as long as possible. With more understanding of the condition and the mutated chromosome, maybe there will be a hope for my children, grandchildren, great-grandchildren. All I can do, though, is stay alive to be a research subject and be a support for my family as they possibly face the same illness.

I've learned so much from my illness, and I have strength enough left to leave behind a legacy of hope, strength, and perseverance. Just as my great-great grandfather spent two months on a boat in pitch darkness playing Lady Bass for his food, I have spent years in my own darkness using music to help me survive my MS. As my daughters and their children deal with their own struggles, I hope they can also learn the Survival Power of Music.

31

Bethany's Legacy of Music

My daughter Bethany and I share the gift of intuition. She's my soul sister, my mini-me. We have deep, philosophical conversations. My relationship with Bethany is very sweet. She gets me, and I get her. We see the things other people miss.

It breaks my heart to know that she has, unfortunately, inherited the broken chromosome. She has a very severe case of Lupus (SLE), and she's beginning to also show signs of MS. Even though her Lupus makes her tired beyond her years, Bethany generously gives of her borrowed energy to make the three-hour trip from Tuscaloosa, Alabama, to my house regularly. She's an executive for a large employment firm in Tuscaloosa, which means she is on call 24/7 to troubleshoot personnel problems. Her routine has become driving to Nashville on Friday night and leaving my house on Monday before dawn. Bethany's busiest job, however, is raising three young, active children: twins—Isabella and Christian—and their big sister, Dalayla.

Recently, I decided to hand down Lindsey's piano, which I still had, to Bethany. She was visiting and her daughter Bella was using my elegant Spanish guitar Lullaby as a drum. Bella adores playing music, whether it be an instrument or a pile of pots and pans, and she had learned that if she hit the guitar hard enough, she could wake up Lullaby's strings without ever touching them. Bethany had rushed to save the guitar from Bella's fists, and she paused with the guitar in her hands and ran her fingers down the strings. Her face glowed the same way it did when she was a child on Christmas morning. Lullaby's music flowed through Bethany's fingers and I could see the magic of music nourish her soul. I knew that magic!

She asked about the odd design of Lullaby's main body. I told her the story of how when I first got sick, a dear friend drew the design and had it custom made in Valencia, Spain. The unique design enables me to rest my head on the carefully-carved curve of the guitar's main body. I shared that no matter how weak I get, I can lay my head on Lullaby and her music soothes my pain away.

After seeing her reaction to music, I asked if she wanted Lindsey's piano.

Bethany had tears in her eyes as she said, "Momma, you don't understand. I really appreciate all the money and time you put into my art training, and I really enjoyed painting and drawing. I know God gave me talent in that area. But through all those years, I really wanted to play the piano. I wanted to play so badly, but you sent Lindsey for lessons. When I was the receptionist, I listened to every lesson. I would watch Mrs. Fargo teach in the front room beside me, and I learned the scales and notes, but I always wanted to know more."

I was shocked. Bethany was so gifted artistically, and we tried to help our daughters play to their strengths. Bethany said art took a back seat to her love for music. At nine years old she did a portrait of my Papi that still hangs in my living room. My artist daughter had wished for music the whole time? I realized I had repeated what happened to my half-sister and me in a way. I prevented my daughter from developing musically, just as I was held back!

We fell into each other's arms, weeping with gratitude of this transformative moment.

I was so thrilled I began pulling all my instruments out. I wanted to be sure she got to touch every string I had ever played. The floor of my living room looked like a repair room in a used instrument store. Bethany was attentive to and excited by the unique sound of each instrument. Her daughter Bella had found her favorite drum, Lullaby, and played along with her mother. Bethany's other two children woke up from their naps and joined us on the floor in the musical playground. Bethany began to play one of my songs by ear on my grandfather's 100-year-old lap autoharp. Her children tried to mimic her on each of their selected strings. My instruments had seen many places—but never those bright faces before. As we say in Tune Town, they had "the look"!

As I watched, I saw Bethany as a child. I was filled with gratitude that I could help pass along the knowledge of the healing power of music to her and her children. Yes, there is a feeling of guilt that just as Papi passed along this broken chromosome to me, I've passed it on to her and my grandchildren, but as I watched them play their music, the worry and guilt melted away. They had music, and they knew the power in it already.

I had a room full of future legacies—each with their own joyful passion for music. I felt that God had pre-chosen that moment to reveal my legacy to me, and the sound of their ragtime-pitched music was so beautiful that my heart knew one thing: my babies knew exactly how to "Sing Me to Heaven." I'd passed on the knowledge of the true power of music to them. Anytime, anywhere their song will fill me with the courage to fly home!

PART VII

From Survivor to Songwriter

"Chords of My Song"
By Carolana Callaway
I'm strumming my song, Lord,
Tryin' to learn the right chords.
I'm strumming my song, Lord,
'Bout to play my last chord home.
Angel's strings will be strumming,
And it's my song they'll be humming.
Gonna know how I served you,
By the chords of my song.

The best thing that ever happened to my writing career was a teaching desk I've named "Lady Lovely." I've had other desks, but Lady Lovely will always be my favorite because it's only with her that I'm able to write creatively and produce my best work. All of my songs have been written at this desk, including my first song, "Blessed By The Master's Hands." This book was born at this desk.

I bought Lady Lovely on one of my commutes from class at Georgia Southern University in Statesboro to our home in Glenville.

We had just returned from Venezuela, and I was struggling with my career shift into teaching and missing Papi back in Venezuela.

One night I was driving home from class with my last $40 in my pocket, praying over the fumes in the gas tank of my tiny canary yellow Ford Fiesta. In front of a once general store now turned junk store, I saw a bright blue object, the color of the sky, which reminded me of the houses in Venezuela that were blue on the bottom half and white on top. My heart jumped! I slowed down the car to get a better look. I couldn't believe my eyes—it was a double-drawer wooden desk with a matching chair. Best of all it was painted in a Venezuelan bright blue color!

I spun the wheel to pull off the road and hurried over to the desk. Writing and music were always a source of freedom for me, and the fact that this writing desk was painted "South American" blue made me think of the freedom of flying in the sky. Lady Lovely had soul in her wood, a deep history, and now she could help me restart my writing career after Venezuela. Feeling this desk under my hands felt like God saying, "It's not over yet. You've got some writing to come."

I paid $20 for it and fit that desk into my tiny little car, tying old, worn ropes around her in the hatchback compartment. Most of it hung out of the car as I drove home.

Lady Lovely has been moved to so many houses, to so many rooms, but as long as we're together, my heart feels right and I'm able to write. Even on a cloudy day my view will still be lovely because I have the secure foundation of Lady Lovely beneath me.

Not only does she provide a firm foundation for me, Lady Lovely gives me soft comfort when my back and legs ache. She has a bar across the bottom, just right for propping my legs when my back hurts.

I now live in Lewisburg, Tennessee, which is near Nashville, and I made sure that Lady Lovely has found her final throne in my home. She sits beneath a triple picture window overlooking my neighbor's beautiful botanical rock garden. Our two rolling well-manicured yards form a mini pastoral view. From the upper corners of the windows, I will soon see sunrise peek in. The sunrise will be framed by the centuries old, beautiful and stately trees that reach above the second floor of the house. This is where I'm most at peace because I feel free.

Lady Lovely has given me hope, strength, and passion through the years, and it's with those intentions that I begin the final section of my book. I hope that developing this book with Lady Lovely as my base will ensure my legacy will live on even when I am gone.

Songwriter's Freedom Song

"Wild Seeds"
By Carolana Callaway and Mark Cawley
Wild seeds
Strong as they have to be
Beauty in a wild country
Even if nobody sees
Every little seed's a dream
Wild seeds
'Little tougher than the rest
Have to be to be the best
Growing straight and tall and true
Oh what a little wild seed can do

Our house in Molena, Georgia, was often called a Jewel. It was built in 1862 and had 12-foot ceilings, original stucco walls and lighting fixtures, and original fireplaces and mantels in the two front parlors. So why couldn't my heart find a place to write in such a grand old house? My only dream was to write, but I couldn't just sit down and write. My heart ached for more simplicity, more freedom. My soul longed for more solitude. To do my best writing, I needed more silent moments.

My need for change hit me like hammers against a solid stone wall. Changes had to be made in my life! If I wanted to save my writer's life, I would have to move. With my Multiple Sclerosis, moving seemed impossible. But living in the Jewel of Molena made writing impossible. Somehow I had to make the move for change.

I packed like the Beverly Hillbillies and moved away from my large, busy house in Atlanta, Georgia. Brian stayed behind in Atlanta. I needed time alone to pray and write. The tiny house I had intended to buy in East Tennessee was condemned the day I arrived. But one hour later, God led me to a tiny, secluded cabin on the Tennessee River. Built completely of hand-hewn cedar longs, the inside smell welcomed me to my new writing place. It was one room with a sleeping loft. The size didn't matter because it had a giant picture window that overlooked the Tennessee River. I couldn't wait to get my old writing desk centered below it.

After midnight, I finally got everything unpacked including my desk. Exhausted from the day's ordeal, I barely noticed a black pencil case that I had dropped. Inside the case was a bottle filled with wildflower seeds. I had carried the bottle of seeds with me all over the world. It was priceless to me!

Decades before, a wise, elderly lady had given me that bottle of wild seeds. She told me to save the wild seeds to be scattered wherever my heart found freedom—that would be my heart's final home. "No matter where your heart may wander," she said,

"It will someday find a home where your wild seeds will feel freedom." She also told me to gather and add more wild seeds all along my life's trail. She said, "Your wild seeds hold those special dreams that only you can dream… and those dreams are what make you unique. Only in your own uniqueness can your heart find the freedom to soar!"

I thought about her words. My new address was Eagle Nest Island. Once there, I set my inner eagle—my music—free. The solitude and silence allowed the voice of my heart to become louder and clearer. Like an eagle, my heart finally had the freedom to soar! My heart had found its home, and now my wild seeds could finally be scattered. Those tiny seeds had finally been set free.

I was free to start writing a song of tribute to my own Wild Seeds. It became a type of personal freedom song. As I wrote, I realize that my wild seeds are what make my life interesting. They make me unique. Without a few lived dreams here and there, my life can become very boring and routine.

To live my life to the fullest, I have to be brave enough to take care of my songwriter dreams. Each of my songwriting dreams lives inside my "wild seeds, strong as they have to be!"

33

Where Do I Go From Here?

"I Got This"
By Carolana Callaway, Dennis Dearing, and Eva Wilson
That's when our Lord says:
I've got this!
Have faith, and do your best.
I've got this!
My grace will do the rest.
I've got this!
I promise,
I've got this.

When I began writing this book, little did I know that this chapter might actually be my final chapter!

In the last few years I have fought many battles against my Marburg's/Malignant Multiple Sclerosis. Doctors have been amazed at my ability to outlive my original prognosis of three to five years given in 2007. I too am amazed but know that without my faith there would be no courage to fight.

I have a growing awareness that courage alone just isn't enough to fight when your body is exhausted. I sat in shock as my compassionate neurologist explained in a very sweet, sister-like manner that the forewarned decline was now my present condition. New lesions continue to appear both within my brain and on my spinal cord where the nerves go to the lungs. The most frightening issue is that with each increase of lesions my insurance company threatens to withdraw benefits for my life-supporting IVIG (IGG) therapy. They are only willing to pay a certain amount per treatment and only as long as I am showing improvement or the lesion growth is being detained. It's a battle we have to fight every 21 days, and we just pray they will continue to pay as long as possible.

Additionally, without proper oxygen supply to my blood and muscles, all my body systems are becoming increasingly exhausted. If my nerve signals grow any slower, I could just pass out to my death. Plus, as my body is worn out, the horrific spasms will continue to grow in intensity. CBD oil helps, but it is not healing me. I still have MS.

In September 2018, I had a two-hour long seizure out of nowhere. After taking CBD oil, I had not had a seizure in months, and suddenly, I had one big enough that my doctor was surprised I'd survived at all. I feel very fortunate to be alive, but my doctor said I would probably still have aftershock seizures intermittently for weeks.

"A lot of people's hearts would not be able to withstand that long of a seizure."

Do I have a strong heart? Maybe my will to survive is strong enough, partially thanks to my lifelong relationship with music.

My doctor told me that after a seizure as large as the one I had, it could take months for the dulled, numb feeling to go away. The fear of it happening again is instilled in you, and when you add a flurry of medications with unknown side effects, it's just a salad you don't want to toss. I was so flat-lined that when I finally did laugh, it was a surprise to my husband and me. Each new point of deterioration reminds me that just because I hope for more time doesn't mean I'm granted it. Seeing is more difficult for me now, and I can't read or interpret music anymore. I know they are notes, but my brain can't translate it in my mind to sound, and my fingers can't play the notes. As hard as it is to see my body suffer, it is so much harder to see my mind and my relationship to music change.

I am so sad for my family. I have raised three beautiful daughters and two adopted children in Ghana, West Africa. They are all adults and married now. Christy loves medicine, Bethany won her first oil painting award at the age of nine, and Lindsey performs dramas in the theaters of Chicago and London. I am also a grandmother of seven wonderful grandchildren. My heart breaks for them. I will miss so many of their special life moments. At all their milestone events, my "Proud Nana" chair will be empty. The truth is, while fighting the later stages of this disease, that chair has been left empty far too often.

As words like "terminal," "advanced," and "hospice care" are spoken around me, the reality of my end stares at me right in the face daily. I must let go of my soldier-like courage to fight and embrace the white garment of surrender. I must follow Jesus' example when he prayed: "Father into your hands I commit myself." I have put myself into the hands of Jesus. I lie down. I surrender myself. I rest myself. Like a weary child, I am so willing to lay my head in his lap and just surrender to the softness of his comforting hands as they soothe my exhausted body. I am returning to the same loving Jesus I would meet at my childhood swing. Once there, he would calm my crushed heart and bruised body, after yet another daily abuse episode. He would come to me as a sweet lullaby of comfort. Yet, I know that the sound of his voice in Heaven will be sweeter and more comforting than any lullaby we can image here on earth. The human heart has yet to hear such a sweet sound here on earth, because it can only be heard in Heaven.

I know that when I lay my head in his lap, I will no longer be chained to the long nights of excruciating spasm pains. I will leave that pain down here on earth, and I will move toward those sweet Heaven sounds of his voice.

For this reason, I wrote the song "Sing Me To Heaven." I want all my family and friends to celebrate my freedom to fly home to Heaven and leave my pain behind. With each joyful song, the singer will be blessed in his or her own heart, too. All the singing and dancing and stomping will not only celebrate my home-going but also each person's life. A celebration song cannot be sung without bringing joy to each voice singing it. For it is a joy-song!

So come on, join in! You are invited to my home-going celebration. Wear your best stomping boots because I love a loud song! Get that beat going! I want to go home with an all-day-singing with *dinner-on-the-ground. Just save me a pair of fried chicken wings—cause I'm getting ready to fly!

*This is a southern term for a covered-dish picnic groups share together outside.

Sing Me to Heaven

"Sing Me to Heaven"
By Carolana Callaway
Sing me to heaven,
With the joy of your songs,
With bright, happy faces,
Sing out loud and real strong.
This ain't gonna be,
A sad, somber occasion.
Come ready to sing,
Of my life's celebrations.
I want you to:
Sing ... dance ... and joyfully shout!
'Cause you know:
That's all my life's been about!
Join hands together:
Smile ... Hug ... in a circle love!
'Cause you know
I'll be smiling from up above!
Just sing me to heaven,
With joy of your songs ...

Oh yes ... come on and ...
Please sing me to heaven,
With the joy of your songs.

For most people, death may be life's greatest fear. To me, death brings my life's greatest, joyful song. As I watch my MS melt my life away, I again face it with song because a simple song of praise can melt any of my fears of death away. How does that work for me? I believe that each time a Christian (one of his very own children) is singing praise to him they are rewarded with a glimpse of heaven. That peek into heaven is what we call joy, but joy is just a practice for our hearts to be ready for living forever in heaven. Each glance of heaven causes my heart to jump with joyful excitement. That joyful excitement is what I call a heart-song. When each song is written and completed, I feel that same emotion, and through my songs I want all my friends and family to celebrate my life. While each one is joyfully singing, I pray that each of their hearts will feel a glimpse of heaven and they too will echo: Sing Me to Heaven.

I now must turn my face toward heaven and hear the music in the winds of courage that will soon take me there. God hears my heart's song, and his great physician power comes down and calms the bone-breaking pain of my spasms. Every night, he hears my painful calls and brings to me his musical miracles. In those rare painless, peaceful moments, my heart feels another piece of heaven. I cannot tell you how my life will end, but I can tell you that God will be there to Sing Me to Heaven.

Timeline of Events

1958	Year of birth, living in Louisiana with Papi, Momma, and Momma's grandmother
1960	Momma goes back to Birmingham to her ex-husband, remarries back into the Fosters
1961-1974	Foster care years
1974	Marriage to Donald when foster care ends
1975	Christy is born
1976	Graduate with Associates Degree of Science in Nursing from Samford
1976-1981	Work as ER nurse
1980	Bethany is born
1983	Move to Venezuela as Southern Baptist Missionary working in journalism
1984	Lindsey is born
1988	Complete coursework for Doctorate in Anthropology and Latin American Studies at University of Simon Bolivar

Sing Me to Heaven

1988	Flee Venezuela
1988	Receive teaching license from Georgia Southern college in Statesboro, Georgia
1989	Accept position as Regional Migrant Education Coordinator in Southeastern Georgia
1991	Thanksgiving—Diagnosed with cervical cancer, aggravated by the stress of domestic abuse, doctor refuses to do surgery until I am no longer living with Donald
1991-1992	Christmas—surgery done, I live with friend to recover for a couple months, stress from divorce proceedings leads to cancer recurring twice more in following year
1992	Divorce from Donald, move to Atlanta Area
1992	Married Brian and lived in Atlanta area in Monroe, Georgia, for a couple years
1992	Papi disappears
1997	Brian is transferred to Washington, DC
1997	Begin studying International Law at George Mason near DC
1999	First assignment with the UN to Bolivia as a field reporter, Lindsey stays with me during the summer

• Timeline of Events •

2000	Transfer to University of United Nations to finish law degree in International and Human Rights Law
2001	Brian is transferred to Fort Jackson, South Carolina
Sept 2001	Pentagon hit in September 11th attacks, area of pentagon is the offices Brian worked in, his secretary and many of our friends are killed
2003	Move back to DC, I graduate with Doctorate of International Human Rights Law degree
2006	Trip to Ghana, when entire left leg becomes numb
2007	Diagnosed with MS, original prognosis given of 3-5 years left to live, end of work with UN
2008-2009	Begin songwriting career, two summers of Write About Jesus songwriting program in St. Charles, Missouri
2009	Receive Story Songs Award for song, "Blessed by the Master's Hands"
2010	Brian retires and we moved back to Molena, Georgia
2010-2012	Speer Stamps-Baxter school of music 2010 and 2011 summer intensity program

2010-2012	The Elijah School of Advanced Performance after Stamps-Baxter School of Music with Speer and Gaither approval (held at First Nazarene Church in Brentwood, Tennessee)
2011	St. Patrick's Day—I move to Decatur County, Tennessee. In September, I move to Franklin, Tennessee, to be closer to Nashville and my doctors and the songwriting culture of Nashville
2008-2015	Intense search for biological mother
Jul 2015	Find biological mother in a nursing home in Birmingham, Alabama
Apr 2016	Momma passes away
Jul 2016	Aunt Tibby passes away
2015-2019	Writing this book

About the Author

CAROLANA CALLAWAY is a former United Nations diplomat who holds a PhD in International Human Rights Law. In 2007, she was diagnosed with Marburg's Multiple Sclerosis (or Malignant MS). She retired from the UN and now lives and writes at her home near Nashville, Tennessee. For further reading about her songwriting career and to hear her songs, visit www.carolanasongs.com or follow her on Facebook @carolanasongs.

www.ingramcontent.com/pod-product-compliance
Lightning Source LLC
Chambersburg PA
CBHW060356080526
44583CB00012B/333